"Ministering among the margins for the last several years, I wish that I had Steve's experience and wisdom to draw from before I began! This is a must-read with anyone wrestling with how and why to answer Jesus' call to come to the table, with practical principles to guide our journey."
Kevin Mast, Executive Director of Hope Barrie Group of Ministries

"This is a wonderful (re)centreing of real human connection for those addressing the deep complexities of poverty."
Laura Solberg, Executive Director of Kentro Christian Network

"She doesn't come for food, she comes to be heard!' 'Steve masterfully paints a portrait of the often overlooked and ignored that today's divisive world needs more than ever. He weaves the words of Jesus that demand us to truly see people and urges us to take the first step in love -a step that could change us and the world forever!"
Byron Bradley, Senior Director of The Mustard Seed

COME TO THE TABLE

Mobilizing the Church to Love on the Margins

Thanks

To John, Matt and the stalwart group of travellers in our book cohort who gave me the motivation to write a second book.

To all of those I journey with in this labour of love—partners, friends, staff and leadership at Centre Street Church.

To my father, Garry, and my friends, Lois, Kevin, Laura, Byron, Wendi and Stan—thank you for taking the time to review these experiences at the table and your investment in them—I appreciate your call and passion because you do the very same thing!

To my bride, Colette, and the love of my life—you are my greatest support always, and I am moved and touched by the sacrifice you made to be my most important editor in bringing this to fruition.

And to our children and grandchildren—you are the light of our lives. May this be a gift to you and a gift to Jesus—a legacy of hope with the call that nothing is more important than what we do to make life better for someone else.

This book is dedicated to the life and memory of
Dr. Bradley D. Friesen.
Brad, you are deeply missed; your fingerprints
are all over this!

Contents

Introduction

Silent hooves wind their way through the forest.
Stripes flicker between the light and the shadow
Tracks left in the soft mud are the only sign she has been here.[1]

These words (at a local zoo) describe an animal called the African Bongo. This large, primarily nocturnal antelope inhabits forests and is native to sub-Saharan Africa. It exhibits complex social interactions and appears suddenly to forage for food before fearfully vanishing back into the dense forests, as if it is mostly invisible.

In this book, we consider individuals who perceive themselves as invisible and are regarded as such by others. We discuss a perspective on poverty that necessitates change; one rooted in understanding that ultimately leads to hope. The word "hope" evokes for me the concept of God noticing people whom society often overlooks. Those deemed invisible (meaning we barely acknowledge their existence) are seen as valuable and precious by Him. In short, God looks kindly on the lowly (Psalm 138:6, NIV). This verse reminds me of a place where a friend of mine serves called the Hope Centre. My friend, Kevin, tells me that the opposite of the word "poverty" is the word "connectedness," and he, along with a small group of mighty warriors, embodies this principle.

Kevin lives in a small city outside of the metropolis of Toronto, Ontario, called Barrie. In its edgier downtown area, you'll find buildings that either have "hope" in their name or convey this concept. The idea surrounding all these references to hope is truly the genesis of this book. Within this context, I invite the reader into two distinct realities. First, in this small yet significant place of potential visibility for people experiencing poverty, where there is an opportunity to be considered, noticed and seen, what would it be like to have other spaces where people seeking connection can come, searching for something entirely different? This book is designed to immerse you, as a reader and a life changer, into a perspective that asks, "What if there is such a place for you to be a part of, and where might that place be?"

Second, visibility and connection are essential to community: a genuine, authentic and beautiful storytelling community where family is created and discovered, leading to real change. This is often described as hope. We will discuss these stories and storytellers as we conclude this book, propelling you into this adventure, and you will see how this intertwines with a conversation about advocating for those considered invisible. We begin by highlighting the importance of others' stories (and, of course, our own) and how these narratives come together to form community.

In these pages, you will discover a place inspired by a community I found years ago in Barrie. In this place, individuals from a harsh and unforgiving street would enter a small yet functional space where God was tangibly present. Over a bowl of chili or whatever was the donation du jour, words were shared, stories were told, prayers were offered and people felt heard. Their eyes met and they were loved and acknowledged, perhaps for the very first time. Do you see what God sees? Do you want to? Come to the table—a warm invitation. Everyone has gathered around a table; this one, however, you will never want to leave.

Chapter One

Do You See What I See?

"The poor you will always have with you,
but you will not always have me"
(Matthew 26:11, NIV)

Jesus said, "A man was going down from Jerusalem to Jericho when robbers attacked him. They stripped him of his clothes, beat him, and went away, leaving him half dead. A priest happened to be going down the same road, and when he saw the man, he passed by on the other side. Similarly, a Levite, when he came to the place and saw him, passed by on the other side. But a Samaritan, as he travelled, came to where the man was; and when he saw him, he felt pity for him. He approached him and bandaged his wounds, pouring on oil and wine. Then he placed the man on his donkey, brought him to an inn, and took care of him. The next day, he took out two denarii and gave them to the innkeeper. 'Look after him,' he said, 'and when I return, I will reimburse you for any extra expense you may have'" (Luke 10:30-35, NIV).

Through my work with those on the margins, I have engaged in numerous conversations with individuals about why they should consider serving those experiencing poverty. These church talks—held in hallways and atriums—remain awkwardly imprinted in my mind. However, I have come to realize that this feeling arises from a lack of understanding, along with the question of how someone can be part of something they don't comprehend. Something they cannot see?

We live in a time when little remains unspoken or undebated. I find it interesting when people strive to convince others that they hold no prejudices when, in fact, societal discrimination exists; at times, it is as pervasive as the air we breathe. I feel this way when discussing individuals who experience poverty. Jesus is remarkably insightful and powerful in unsettling the things we want to hide—our perceptions, judgments, and fears. He shared stories and parables that cut to the core of something, and the story of the Good Samaritan is no exception!

A man lies battered and bleeding in an ancient thoroughfare, and what is glaringly sad is the extent to which others take pains to walk on the far side of a wide street. We love the walls we erect, don't we? Yes, I can hear your voices, your objections: "Okay, just because this is your thing, your cause, why does it have to be mine?" And the truth is that you have no obligation to serve those on the margins, but try as you might, you cannot ignore them! Because, if you think this is a problem or issue you do not need to be involved in, you are not only that one person with your head down, walking quickly on the other side of the street to something much more comfortable, but you are also walking away from what is central to the heart of Jesus.

I have dedicated myself to this mission, so at times, it is challenging for me to see the other side of the story. On a cold COVID afternoon, a group of individuals distribute box lunches through a side door of a church. Among this group is a dear older woman, so kind yet relatively uninformed. She engages with a man of about 35, whom we'll call Sam. Sam is dishevelled, wearing a threadbare jacket and exuding the aura of the street. He is an affable man: friendly, gregarious, and open. He interacts with the older woman and regales her with his life and stories. Somewhere in this conversation, she says, "Really, your only problem is that you need a job."

We love pat answers, and when we make assumptions about things we cannot understand or relate to, we cause harm and exhibit arrogance. This woman was not cruel; she was uneducated and unaware of this reality. Similarly, the reason I may hesitate to become more deeply involved is my fear of delving too deeply; I don't want to identify with behaviours and lifestyles that I don't comprehend. It simply feels far too uncomfortable, and how sympathetic can I be to what I might perceive as laziness or mere excuses to piece a life together?

While Jesus was in Bethany, at the home of Simon the Leper, a woman approached him with an alabaster jar of expensive perfume, which she poured on his head as he reclined at the table. When the disciples saw this, they were indignant. "Why this waste?" they asked. "This perfume could have been sold at a high price and the money given to the poor." Aware of this, Jesus said to them, "Why are you bothering this woman? She has done a beautiful thing for me. The poor you will always have with you, but you will not always have me" (Matthew 26: 6-11, NIV). This is an often-quoted yet rarely understood verse.

Prioritizing the needs of individuals experiencing poverty is a topic often sincerely discussed by many advocates who genuinely care about helping those in need. This indicates that we feel an obligation to act; Jesus, the Book of Proverbs and various parts in Scripture address the experience of poverty hundreds of times. Consequently, there is a clear sense that we must act—but what exactly does this involve? What should we do? A better question is, what are we being asked to focus on, or on whom?

Let us envision a story together before returning to a lovely illustration of a woman with expensive perfume. Here is a typical depiction of a city: it shows trash bins, alleys and dumpsters. You walk out of your backyard gate and you are surprised by what you see along your back fence. You see a man tightly wrapped in a plastic sheet, with remnants of food and tattered clothing scattered around—a backpack, a sleeping bag and a shopping cart. In my work, I mentor others to avoid responding with fear when they encounter something like this because it is easy to see a situation and not recognize a person. The goal is to strive to emulate Jesus with our love and understanding, but too often, we do the opposite. Prejudice and a sliver of fear emerge, and perhaps we realize that compassion is easy to discuss but more challenging to put into action... so you tell that man to leave, to go elsewhere, and maybe you wonder if you could have approached that differently.

I believe that the key is not what occurs, but the person—the Who. We observe this here and in the example of the woman pouring perfume on Jesus' head, where the people's response is not to a who but to a what! This highlights how Jesus handles the reactions and prejudices in this story. For context, this is believed to be another account of the same story in John 12, where the woman's identity is described as Mary, the sister of Lazarus, part of the family who were close friends of Jesus. It is thought she performs this act to thank Jesus for what He has done for these friends, particularly the raising of Lazarus, and she also does it to prepare Jesus for burial. This act is, in fact, extravagant. It would have been normal in their day to anoint a guest in your home with common household oil, but Mary uses a costly perfumed ointment to anoint Jesus.

Those gathered view this as an opportunity to condemn a beautiful and intimate act of love by arguing that it could have been used to help the poor. It is clear from this context that people experiencing poverty are neither their priority nor the focus of their care—these individuals are seen as outcasts in society, perceived as being beneath the social status of those making the comments. Jesus' correction, "The poor you will always have with you," serves as a prod, suggesting that if they genuinely cared, there is much they could do. This commentary reveals their failure to focus not on a problem but on individuals, prompting the statement, "If you genuinely cared about them, you would do something beautiful for them, just as this simple woman is doing for her

Lord and friend, who is soon to face his death."

The question raised by this Scripture and our story in the alley is to what extent this is a problem for me, something that I should engage with? If that is an honest objection or inquiry for you, then what follows is a detailed account based on these stories. I must ask, is that even a question? Are your concerns and prejudices rooted in a fear of pursuing something that would take you too far from your comfort zone, which is a place of pronouncements like, "Could this have been sold and the money given to the poor?" Earlier in this chapter, I mentioned that we can't identify with behaviours and lifestyles we can't understand; a lack of understanding does feed into our excuses. If we don't get too close, we have already decided not to understand.

In relation to this, you might choose to merge this decision with a sense of calling. If you don't feel called to this area of need, then you must feel called to something else. Thus, your reasoning might suggest that it makes sense for you to maintain some distance and not worry about what you can't understand because, after all, you don't need to. Conversely, what if you considered it this way—what if it isn't about what you understand regarding people, and it isn't about waiting for the right action, but rather about stepping out, loving people and allowing God to grant you a ministry where your previous reasons were merely excuses? It is a call to and for the few, because many don't truly engage with this mindset. In the thinking that leads to action regarding those on the margins, many prefer a path that the majority follow—one that is wide and comfortable. The exception is those who embrace a road less travelled.

There is a poem by Robert W. Service, called "The Lone Trail," that tells this tale. It speaks of a road less travelled, a path of courage, and a way of being set apart.

"The trails of the world are countless, and most of the trails have been tried.

You tread on the heels of many, till you come where the ways divide.

And one lies safe in the sunlight, and the other is dreary and wan,

Yet you look aslant at the Lone Trail, yet the Lone Trail leads you on."[2]

What if our fears point to our most significant opportunities? What if our discomfort reveals where we are destined to be? What if taking a step in a particular direction, toward a specific person, represents the "road less travelled" that has a significant impact for Christ and His kingdom? I believe there's a reason you're reading this—perhaps it's your turning point. As the poem indicates, there are two paths to choose from. We should raise our heads high, relying on God to give us the courage needed to fulfill our mission and calling, while moving forward with love and compassion. The initial step is life-changing, paving the way for the next one and the one after that, making it impossible to look back. Something prevents you from veering away from this new path each time. Is it God? What if you are like a woman I have come to know? She is shy and uncertain, and eventually, she relinquishes her excuses, as they do not lead her toward any path or direction. She arrives at a musty and worn little space, where we are attempting to cobble together a gathering for a handful of homeless people, and she brings a plate of brownies. The burning in her heart, the thing she has ignored for so long, is to find a people she could love, a group she could serve, and the cry of her heart is, "Are these my people?"

Walking the Objections

I would love to share a little test case or experiment for you to reflect on and explore why you might not feel the urge to engage more deeply. I completely understand that you might genuinely believe that God is guiding you in a different direction; still, it's worth considering that what you perceive as their issue could be something to reflect on personally. Here are some common challenges I often encounter while supporting individuals on their journey to discover their calling:

- How can I possibly help so many?

- What kind of difference can I make?

- Is success truly achievable? What do I know about it, and what can I contribute to an issue as vast as homelessness?

- Am I sympathetic to their plight—do I even care? Why do they appear so helpless? Can't they find a way to help themselves?

- What if they take advantage of me?

- How can I overcome my fears about this population?

This is what I do with dozens of people each year during training and orientation. It is essential to move away from specific objections and focus instead on what we discussed earlier in the chapter: people, not problems. Regardless of what you ultimately decide God is calling you to, the focus and intent must remain the same. Prioritizing people over problems, worries or things that intimidate us, truly embodies the spirit of love. In every situation we encounter, we are to respond with love. "Follow God's example[...]as dearly loved children and walk in the way of love, just as Christ loved us and gave Himself up for us as a fragrant offering and sacrifice to God" (Ephesians 5:1-2 NIV).

I oversee a café space in our church that serves hot meals to about 500 people each week. This work requires many volunteers and individuals to engage directly with those in poverty, on the margins, and the working poor. Some bag bread, some cook food, some serve meals and several sit at the tables with our guests. Every role is essential and serves a critical purpose as we strive to create an environment of welcome, relationship and belonging; the gathering is truly the centrepiece. Our model, of course, is Jesus, and I often highlight that Jesus spent much time eating in others' places—in their homes, at their tables, looking them in the eye and breaking bread—because this very posture promotes a unique type of intimacy and vulnerability.

People come to us to volunteer and engage in this work. Some feel a strong call to make a difference in the lives of the poor, while others join because our church promotes it widely, searching for a community they can connect with—could this be them? We invite those with a desire to love and serve to see what we do and to discover what God may be saying to each of them as individual servants, along with what He may be calling them to do. If they choose to stay with us and commit to volunteering (and most do), it is not because their objections have been addressed in an academic dialogue. Instead, it is because they have heard the stories that led them to the heart of a person and to the way of love.

Thomas feels like a complete failure, and his entire family seems to share that sentiment. Once, he had a good job, a lovely wife and a house on a nice street. Then, shadows of emotional turmoil crept in, pressures at work mounted and he found himself spending time at a casino. Before long, he spent every evening at VLT terminals and game tables, with a glass of scotch, causing all his paycheques to vanish, along with his wife and home. Now, he shows up for a warm meal in the north wing of our church, seeking a sense of community.

Sara faces challenges due to mental illness. As a result, nearly everyone she encounters tends to avoid her. She lost a child amidst her pain—the details remain unclear—but she carries a scrapbook filled with pictures of the little girl she lost. She is searching for someone, anyone who will listen to her tragic story. Here in a church café, she doesn't come for food; she comes to be heard. Week after week, she finds other caring women (we call them volunteers, but in truth, they are angels), and the three of them sit together, listen, embrace and, perhaps, Sara finds a family after all.

The two vignettes above focus on individuals being served, while also highlighting volunteers who recognize what lies within a soul—not in societal philosophies, but in suffering and hope. Robert also arrived, searching for a way to serve at his church and trying to find his place while grappling with many personal traumas of his own. Initially filled with skepticism, he was not convinced as we attempted to mentor him in our philosophy of life change, based on John 10:10: "The thief comes only to steal and kill and destroy, but I have come that you might have life and have it to the Full" (NIV). His focus lay on philosophy rather than "story," and he left in anger. However, one day he returned—contrite, broken and homeless—ready to embrace this message of hope. We often witness this; God witnesses it on a larger scale, offering a warm welcome with open arms.

My point is that, although there is room for discussion on various issues, topics and philosophies as needed, overcoming objections is not the primary means of cultivating a heart and passion for serving individuals experiencing poverty. In medical administration at hospitals and with support workers, a formula exists for administering prescription drugs, which is as follows: right patient, right drug, right dose, right route, right time, right documentation, right response. The purpose of this is to recognize that a specific plan is developed for someone receiving lifesaving drugs, and the medical worker must be aware of it. Therefore, it focuses on the individual, providing the appropriate assistance with the right amount of support, noting what has occurred and responding accordingly.

Imagine you're a guest. I sit across from you as you share your story or struggle. I consider one simple way to show I care: offering encouragement, a prayer, a thought or an idea. It's just that one simple thing—I don't know you well enough to suggest a solution. I want you to realize that I'm here for you. I need to be sensitive about how I express this. It's your life and I can't truly grasp your feelings or circumstances. Have I earned the right to engage or even hear your story? Is this the right time? I listen closely, showing my compassion. I recall your name and the information you provided. As I push my chair back to close the space, I leave you with a parting word, a smile or a nod that signifies my presence! It is only after this interaction that I, the listener, entertain my objections.

It dates back a few years, but I love Mark Burnett's The Bible television miniseries. Much like the current series, The Chosen, it was also celebrated for its grit, realism and authenticity. This series led to a film called Son of God.[3] In this separate movie, Jesus calls the disciples into a boat and joins them in the activity of hauling nets aboard, which are overflowing with fish. As the oily, wet fish, numbering in the hundreds, slide along the deck, Jesus talks to his friends about what it means to be fishers of men. They wonder about this term, and Peter asks, "What will we do?" Jesus replies, "Oh...just change the world." Let's embark on this journey together, believing in its potential to transform us. Although it may involve some effort, it can change the world!

Jesus is our example! He seeks the lost, broken and hurting; He finds them, cares for them, releases them from oppression, binds up their wounds and leads them home to a place of belonging. The other night, I was awakened and God graciously gave me a picture of our café as a representation of the home to which God is calling us—the Kingdom He is building, embodying all the things mentioned in the words above, on Earth as it is in Heaven. The phrases "release from oppression" and "binding up wounds" originate from the prophet Isaiah and are later quoted by Jesus: "The Spirit of the Sovereign Lord is upon me, because the Lord has anointed me to proclaim good news to the poor. He has sent me to bind up the broken-hearted, to proclaim freedom for the captives and release from darkness for the prisoners[...]to comfort all who mourn[...]to bestow a crown of beauty instead of ashes, the oil of joy instead of mourning, and a garment of praise instead of a spirit of despair" (Isaiah 61: 1-3, NIV).

In conclusion, we can address the fears associated with our calling to bring "good news for the poor" by showing compassion and helping others build the confidence to step forward and be recognized. They can find a sense of security and safety, reassured that God will be their home. Are we willing to be the ones who improve the situation? Can we become the 'game changer' they require? I urge you to join me in this rescue operation.

Chapter Two

Your Place at the Table

"Always weigh the cost of a goal against the expense of reaching it"

Sir Ernest Shackleton[4]

Gather at the Table

What does it mean to look into someone's eyes? I mean, really look—not just a casual glance followed by averted eyes, gazing out a window or down at the tabletop. I wonder if you have ever had a different experience. The gaze into eyes that you couldn't look away from—eyes as deep as wells, eyes that you felt truly knew you. It can be frightening to gaze into the eyes of someone we believe knows us well enough to see deeply within. Who would ever look at us, look into us like that? Your personal spiritual journey and its resonance will determine whom I refer to; naturally, the answer (as in every Sunday school lesson) is Jesus. When Jesus looks into our eyes, He does more than simply look; He sees, probes and understands. It is a penetrating gaze, not a casual glance; the Son of God does not use His eyes or look into yours as if He were reading a street sign. It is an examination that sees deeply, even burning into those of us who meet his gaze.

Eugene Peterson said, "Our first response to the prospect of such an examination would be to run for cover. Yet we need not. There is mercy and generosity in the honest, unflinching gaze of our Lord. If His look burns, it is the fire of Love, and it burns so that it may warm us."[5] This experience mirrors that of the disciple of Jesus, Nathanael. As he approaches the Lord. Jesus says, "Here truly is an Israelite in whom there is no deceit" (John 1:47, NIV). Nathanael hears of Jesus, Nathanael comes and Jesus sees. We understand several aspects of Jesus: His kindness, goodness, soul-stirring stories, and passion for food.

The Messiah, in his human nature, enjoyed gathering around food. Walking down dusty roads, he picks things from various types of foliage to eat; He plucks the ends of grain stalks. You can be sure He had some of the leftover bread and fish. Jesus spent considerable time dining at people's homes. The following verses exemplify such occasions: "Zaccheus—come down immediately, I must stay at your House today" (which culturally included sharing a meal). Also, "Then Levi held a great banquet for Jesus at his house, and a large crowd of tax collectors and others were eating with them" (Luke 5: 29). And another time, "When one of the Pharisees invited Jesus to have dinner with him, He went to the Pharisee's house and reclined at the table" (paraphrase of Luke 19).

Dining in someone's home cultivates a sense of intimacy and connection. While putting on airs may create a more formal atmosphere, sitting at the same level helps lower one's guard. In the ancient world, people often sat on cushions on the floor, reclining at the table, breaking bread together and looking into one another's eyes. Perhaps, just perhaps, in this posture, a wall comes down, a glance is exchanged, and a more knowing word is spoken. Part of the reason Jesus sat in people's homes and at their tables was to get to know them and establish eye contact. In the previous chapter, I introduced you to a café located within a church. No frills: just a couple of tables, several chairs, a kitchen, and coffee urns. In the church where I serve, we have undertaken a wide variety of initiatives to help people and get to know them. We distribute food in hampers, give out free clothing and assist individuals in paying rent; yet nothing is more important or influential than the experience of doing what Jesus did when he said, "I must eat at your house today!"

It's afternoon, and I'm sitting in my car in the west-side parking lot of a massive church where I recently started working. I have served as a local pastor in suburban areas and in homeless shelters. This is the first time I've been hired to bridge these two worlds. I'm sitting in my Kia, having been here for a while, feeling a bit anxious about going to work. I have a considerable task ahead of me, and while I've been doing well launching this initiative, I've sensed that something is missing. But I do not, for the life of me, know what that is. Then it hits me... I notice a sign in the parking lot that says, "Visitor Parking." As someone who truly believes that God has a voice and that you can hear it because he speaks to you, I discover the missing piece: "Steve—the people you serve are like people trapped in visitor parking; they go from place to place, seeking welcome and belonging and some semblance of a home, and in a café space where all you need is a table—they will be visitors no more."

Consider the following scenario. The CEO of a Fortune 500 company sits in a resplendent office. His life revolves around material possessions, power and prestige. Today, however, he reflects on his actions and the things he has left undone. He thinks about the people he has known, those he has hurt, and those he has loved. His thoughts wander to his best friend—a man who has long since passed, as close as a brother. He calls his assistant and asks her to have his team investigate whether any surviving members of his friend's family exist; he wishes to pay tribute, offer thanks and honour his friend. A few days later, the assistant brings a young, dishevelled man into the CEO's extravagant office. This young man is his friend's grandson; he is homeless and in rags. He grips tightly onto a backpack that is his only possession. The CEO says, "Wherever you have been, whatever you have done, it makes no difference. Your grandfather was my dearest friend." Even now, this rich man holds him in his heart, and out of love for his dearest friend, he says, "I invite you to move into my mansion, work in my company, and you will eat at my table." And this man, outcast, marginalized and broke, says, "Who am I that you would ever notice a bottle picker like me?"

The inspiration for this story is drawn from a friendship depicted in God's Word: David and Jonathan were as close as two friends could be. Their friendship is rooted in love and tested through adversity, as seen in 2 Samuel 9:8, NIV. In this passage, David decides he must do right by his friend Jonathan and Jonathan's family. I imagine there are times when David (a man after God's own heart) reflects on the mistakes he made and the sins he committed, seeking redemption in all its forms. Thus, he searches for a lost family member without realizing he is an outcast—someone on the margins. This person, named Mephibosheth, says to the king, when brought before him, "What is your servant, that you should notice a dead dog like me!" He is called forth, this one with a strange name, and, like our story of the CEO and his friend's grandson, is granted a position beyond his wildest imagination and expectation. I love this story and have taught from it often over the years. It is a prophetic narrative of what Jesus does for outcasts, prostitutes, tax collectors and Pharisees. He invites them to the table.

The table is a place of safety, discovery and hope. This concept of a table—how Jesus used it and how our café utilizes it—as a space of welcome, relationship and belonging, represents what God does for each of us. He invites all His children to join him at his table for eternity. It reminds me of an idea the late Brennan Manning had for a book where, during the US Civil War, a slave owner breaks all the social mores of his day and invites his slaves to eat at the table with his family. How radical and life-changing for both the overseers and the slaves! Something that was never done changed perspectives, rules and expectations, transitioning to love, grace and hope! I have spent considerable time discussing the table, as I'm trying to move away from prejudices, from the "can't" and the "won't," and present the case that the aim is not to find a way to get to know the poor or a plan for overcoming your fears, but to be present and love!

A Rescue Operation

Sir Ernest Henry Shackleton (born February 15, 1874) was an Anglo–Irish Antarctic explorer who prepared for what became the Imperial Trans-Antarctic Expedition of 1914–1917. The expedition faced disaster when its ship, the Endurance, became trapped in pack ice and ultimately sank in the Weddell Sea off Antarctica on November 21, 1915. The crew survived by camping on the sea ice until it disintegrated. In this greatest rescue operation known to mankind, led by Sir Ernest, lifeboats were launched to reach Elephant Island and, ultimately, the South Atlantic Island of South Georgia: enduring a stormy ocean voyage of 1,330km. This story captivates the imagination and, for me, embodies the vision of the rescue we encourage people to undertake for those in need. You might question such intense language. Is it really that serious? Are we truly calling people to a rescue operation?

You turn a corner, searching for a hole-in-the-wall restaurant that someone mentioned. They said it serves the best lobster bisque in town. As you seemingly stumble around, you find yourself in an alley and there it is—halfway down—a door adorned with a painted red lobster. You walk toward it, and to your left, a man bundled in layers of clothing huddles inside a cardboard refrigerator box, bracing against the cool, windy day. You feel your heart tighten, and your breath stops; could this be compassion? A tug of sadness emerges, but also a desire not just to avoid but to act! This surprising reaction pulls you away from the lingering thoughts of the inner city as you look around at one crisis after another, one need after another, and ask, "What can I possibly do?" Perhaps you are suddenly gripped by a different reality that prompts you to recognize the need for rescue and your part in it.

When I reflect on Sir Ernest Shackleton as an idea or illustration related to those living in poverty, I think about walking alongside people and envisioning the possibility of something vastly different in their lives. It is equally essential to encourage you on a journey to engage with the lives of those in greatest need! I see this as a rescue operation for the poor and, in this chapter, I am motivated, inspired and stirred by Sir Ernest Shackleton, who heroically rescued 27 of his crew trapped in the ice of Antarctica, refusing to believe in any other option than safety and the hope of a future life for all!

Elephant Island

Allow me to elabourate on this portrait of a historical event. Elephant Island is an ice-covered, mountainous island off the coast of Antarctica, located in the outer reaches of the South Shetland Islands, in the Southern Ocean. As previously mentioned, in 1916, it was immortalized as the backdrop to an extraordinary survival story from Ernest Shackleton's ill-fated Antarctic expedition. After their ship, Endurance, was lost to the treacherous ice in the Weddell Sea, the 28 crew members were compelled to undertake a perilous escape attempt. In life—and in the narrative of faith—physically-demanding journeys are the essence of true legends. If achievement is not marked by significant effort, some would argue that it is not worth pursuing. Shackleton intentionally avoided the easy path; he sought challenges, believing that only through trials can we refine ourselves like gold. The Old Testament figure, Job, said, "He knows the way that I take and when He has tested me, I will come forth as gold" (Job 23:10, NIV). No matter what we are engaged in—regardless of what we are called to—we need to embrace the concept known as faith, which involves accepting a reality that transcends our perceived capabilities.

I have been struck by the realization that all of life should be a preparation for eternity. Jonathan Edwards, an early church father known for his sermon "Sinners in the Hands of an Angry God," expressed that "This life ought to be spent by us only as a journey toward ... Eternity."[6] Thus, there is a call to reflect on your journey! I am convinced that God has a unique calling for you, which, if not fulfilled, will remain unaccomplished. Therefore, the question is, what is your Elephant Island? To challenge the notion of a mediocre life of faith, what if there is something unique that you are meant to pursue? Pursuing something worthwhile comes at a cost, but the payoff is incredibly significant! You consider the cost and wonder if you have everything needed—and consequently, contemplate what it requires of you, how God fits in and what venture of faith you should undertake without fear, knowing this mission is for you alone! Shackleton said, "Always weigh the cost of a goal against the expense of reaching it."

Polar exploration, in which Ernest Shackleton played a significant role, has a long and brutal history, marked by dark tragedies as well as startling and deeply inspiring successes. However, the costs of achieving these objectives were high. Before Shackleton, there was a group of men who set out across the ice in unprecedented temperatures. They journeyed 70 miles on foot.

"We had spent days in reaching this place through the darkness in cold such as had never been experienced by human beings. We had been out for four weeks under conditions where no man had survived for more than a few days, if that. During this time, we had seldom slept except from sheer physical exhaustion, and every minute we fought for the bare necessities of existence, always in the dark."[7]

Reflect on your Elephant Island and consider what it means to tread the path laid out for you, and inspire and influence others so they may understand that there is a call to faith. Encourage them to embrace it!

The Endurance illustration has occupied my thoughts for a long time. It depicts an adventure undertaken— a ship venturing into the coldest, starkest, most unforgiving place on Earth. Stopped and trapped in ice, a rescue operation unfolds—this is a destination they must reach. For me, Elephant Island symbolizes this rescue for those in need; it represents a goal we must pursue, a path that can be challenging, where successes may sometimes be difficult to find. We cannot give up. Hungry souls sit at tables, hoping (if they dare) for a better opportunity at a different life. It demands all we have, but it is about building a Kingdom—a restoration to a new Heaven and a new Earth—a belief in a Kingdom, where those who have nearly given up will discover what they were always meant to be.

She came to me today, looking broken and weary, seated in one of those walkers with a basic seat. She felt distressed, longing to fly home to reunite with her son and family, hoping I could help make that happen. We support individuals in various ways: a rent cheque here, a food basket there, but we cannot provide airline tickets. She was in deep anguish: first tearful, then sobbing and finally wailing. She took a bus from a shelter to the airport, hoping someone would offer her a free flight before coming to the church. The bane of my existence is the things we cannot do and the answer "no," which comes far too easily and more often than we would like. Yet sometimes a "no" is the best thing, because directing someone to a better resource can change a life. So, I offered what I could: a sandwich, a bottle of water, bus tickets and a prayer. This is life on the ice, trying to guide someone to a better way and a brighter day, knowing that if it's only a sandwich, it's still a sandwich and maybe a step on a path that brings her to what truly matters.

On this journey, where have we reached so far? We began with fears and objections and transitioned to focusing on people rather than problems. Early in this chapter, we gathered at the table and learned that while it requires some personal investment, it simply involves seeing the person and looking into their eyes. Now, it entails establishing an idea—an idea that has the potential to change the world. Whether for the poor or another life-changing mission, we see in the strength of faith that we are part of a new Kingdom—something we are building right now! What strength is needed to achieve this? What drives our passion? It is nothing less than a heart filled with love. What inspires you? Even more profoundly, what if the change is also for you? What will it take to make your heartbeat race? Are you ready to explore where this could lead you?

I am not sure where I read it, but there is a saying that goes, "Know the outcome and you'll see the journey." This chapter focuses on the outcome. I'm here to cheer you on as you work toward the wonderful goal of befriending and, even more importantly, loving others. While considering this outcome, I also wish to illustrate the journey so we can see it clearly. The journey (if you decide to join me) encompasses four commitments. To reach our desired destination, we must consider a place, a community, a call and a story. It is my prayer, as well as my conviction, that by focusing on a person instead of a problem—not someone in poverty, a meal or a winter coat—we will uncover these four components to ignite a passion for the outcome. As I conclude this chapter, I want to help you consider the power of an outcome that changes lives for the better, forever. As we move to Chapter 3, reflect on how love provides the foundation for the four commitments and convictions mentioned above. What draws us to the outcome of a life that looks different for someone in poverty is Jesus Himself. We must focus on empowering others, breaking down any walls of "us versus them" and building an authentic community (life at the table), knowing that what we do must be done together as we share the heart of the Gospel, which is salvation and belonging for everyone!

Our role model in this mission, of course, is Jesus, and what we observe about him is that He is consistently drawn to the marginalized in the society of his day: women, those caught in cycles of poverty and the sick. He is the greatest friend they could ever have. He serves in love as He heals, touches and meets practical needs. He encourages, teaches and challenges those who find themselves in the wrong place, hoping that they might be strengthened to lead, serve and encourage others as well. The very heart of this book—a rescue operation on behalf of the poor—is ensuring that as many people as possible know that God has called each of us to a unique vision and mission that only we can fulfill: preparing others for eternity. Furthermore, there is no doubt that Jesus has called His people to serve those in need. We have already established that we each have different callings; however, we share the same mandate from Jesus: to serve those in need in various capacities. At the heart of creating an authentic community that God intends for His people lies a commitment to sincerely acknowledge everyone's uniqueness and to understand what it means to love people as they are. As followers of Jesus, we must look beyond our own contexts, prejudices and fears, loving both groups and individuals who have been marginalized. We need to consider what it will take to practice welcome, relationship and belonging so that the equality, dignity and family we all desire can become a reality! The woman I described earlier was frail, confused and tearful—possibly facing mental health challenges. Even though I could not provide her with everything she desired, I can offer her compassion, share my love and listen with the ears and heart of Jesus, ensuring that the outcome of her life reflects dignity. In this way, we recognize that she understands better than anyone else what will bring change to her own life and story. In the next chapter, we will explore the four markers of love that highlight this journey.

Chapter Three

What's Love Got to Do with It?

Love, Acceptance and Forgiveness

I read a book by a pastor named Jerry Cook, 'Love, Acceptance and Forgiveness'. Paraphrased from that book is this story: a pastor in the same town as the author succumbed to moral failure, which resulted in his adultery destroying his church and leaving his life and marriage in ruins. After some time, through a restoration process led by those close to him, he remarried, started a new vocation and sought a new church to call home. He visited several churches with his wife, but word had spread, and each time they were turned away at the door. In desperation, he called Jerry and asked if his church would be willing to welcome them. The man shared his journey with Jerry, recounting the devastation the couple felt while searching for a church home. Jerry said, "You come here Sunday morning, and I will welcome you at the door."[8]

This book, read all those years ago, had a profound impact on me regarding the theme of love. It emphasized that, when properly lived out, the church serves as a vital healing force, suggesting that Christ's followers must acknowledge their own brokenness to love, accept and forgive others effectively. What's love got to do with it? That's the critical next question in this important discovery (many of you can likely hear the classic Tina Turner song in your head). The answer, of course, is everything! I used the illustration above from Love, Acceptance and Forgiveness because this concept has grit. It embodies the messiness present in all of us. We all bring our broken selves to the table, asking, begging and pleading to be loved, accepted and forgiven for the places from which we have come.

The love we share with others is the love we also need to receive. The very crux of this whole missional movement finds its foundation in John 10:10: "The thief comes only to steal and kill and destroy, I have come that you might have life and have it to the full" (NIV). My wife and I have lived, breathed and immersed ourselves deeply in this verse; we remind each other when it's 10:10 on the clock, and we pray for the work of our café and for those we serve there. This verse speaks to the plight of those we serve and acts as a reminder to cherish what we view as hidden, flawed and unlovable. In John 10, Jesus addresses a group of misguided and arrogant Pharisees. In the previous chapter, the Lord had healed a man born blind, and they were questioning just who this Jesus thought He was anyway. When the Pharisees asked, "Are we blind too?" they mockingly referred to physical blindness, but Jesus was speaking of spiritual blindness (John 9:40, NIV). Then, Jesus instructs them on who He is and why He came:

"I am the good shepherd. The good shepherd lays down his life for the sheep. The hired hand is not the shepherd and does not own the sheep. So, when he sees the wolf coming, he abandons the sheep and runs away. Then the wolf attacks the flock and scatters it. The man runs away because he is a hired hand and cares nothing for the sheep. I am the good shepherd; I know my sheep and my sheep know me just as the father knows me and I know the father, and I lay down my life for the sheep.' (John 10:11-15, NIV)

The shepherd is a familiar figure in the ancient world. His life is spent doing little else but tending to his flock. As a result, his sheep know and respond to his voice. He leads them to fresh grazing pastures and guards them from wild animals by lying across the entrance to the sheepfold at night, effectively becoming its gate. There are two things at play in John 10: firstly -in the Old Testament, God is often referred to as the Shepherd of Israel , and his chosen leaders are also referred to as the nation's shepherds. Secondly, Jesus now chooses to describe Himself as the true shepherd. When Jesus describes Himself as the true Shepherd, it means that

- There is a close personal relationship between Him and each of His followers
- There is absolute security in Him if we will but choose to see it
- There is a leader in our lives who guides our steps
- There is a constant presence keeping watch over us
- There exists sacrificial love: "I lay down my life for the sheep." (John 10:15, NIV)

Our focus is a movement—the profound concept of a "rescue operation" and your role in it. This movement is rooted in love: the table of invitation becomes more than just a place to eat, it fosters a sense of belonging and community. More importantly, the overarching focus is on creating a space where love and acceptance flourish. When we shift our focus from problems to people, change takes place, accompanied by a softening of the heart. This transformation guides us in understanding what it means to love and enables us to see how that love ignites change within us. There is a call of love, suggesting that all the things we possess that are hidden, flawed or unlovable can indeed be presented and transformed into what is loved, accepted, forgiven and whole. The core message here is that welcome, relationship and belonging are responses to the brokenness and isolation we all face. Despite the messy and uncomfortable circumstances previously mentioned, thanks to the good shepherd, both we and those we encounter will have everything we could ever need, in this life and the next. The imagery of the shepherd helps us comprehend what it means to be seen by our Lord who loves us and inspires us to love others in the same way.

We must understand what we need to be whole in our own lives; as we experience this, we are moved to serve others so that they may also find a pathway to a fuller life in Jesus. What I hope we all see is that we are not simply trying to find people to love and serve, but that what the good shepherd does in, through and for us—the love we feel, the protection, hope and sense of acceptance for who we actually are—leads us to love those we ask God to reveal to us. Consequently, we take this list and apply it personally:

- A desire for a close personal relationship to make a difference in someone else's life.

- Helping someone in great need understand that where trust was absent for much of their life experience, trust is possible because they are seen and loved.

- Jesus will lead us to the person we seek to love and help, serving as a guide, not a hero.

- In our work, as we focus on individuals and their life stories, we recognize this as walking alongside others. Just as Jesus walks with us as a companion, we strive to accompany others.

- Although we may not be perfect, we rise from what we have received to provide care, love, concern and a sense of welcome, connection and belonging.

- We do not lay down our physical lives in the same manner as Jesus did, but we still set aside our agenda, presuppositions and judgment to discover the path to love.

- In the absence of love, we are prepared to provide a shift toward genuine love.

In Chapter 2, I introduced you to four commitments regarding how to view individuals through the lens of love. Once again, these consist of a place, a community, a call and a story. These elements ground us as we move toward the people we include in our response to what it means to give, invest and serve.

A Place

Heaven transcends anything we can imagine on Earth; indeed, it far exceeds our wildest imaginings. Any comparisons we make appear insignificant. Yet, there are meaningful places here, aren't there? In modern psychology, we're often encouraged to visualize a "happy place": an ocean, a forest, a sunset, wilderness, or indulgences like ice cream or decadent chocolate cake. We might refer to these slices of the heavenly (pun intended), and they hold significance because they evoke joy, peace and calm. I have one as well, and I haven't encountered another quite like it.

Let me share the story of this place and how it makes me feel. Alexander MacDonald, a wealthy businessman from Scotland and former president of the Standard Oil Company, was on vacation with his family in beautiful Prince Edward Island. He was so captivated by the area's splendour that he purchased 120 acres of land, on the north shore, which included a section of cleared farmland and a forest. In 1895, he built a sprawling vacation home for his family, naming it "Dalvay-by-the-Sea" after his boyhood home in

Scotland. Construction reportedly cost around $50,000.00 (a fortune at the time), and local building materials were used exclusively. The lower half of the house was constructed with island sandstone in its natural boulder form, while the massive fireplaces were also made from quarried blocks of the famous PEI reddish sand.

My Experience of Place

It was our honeymoon, and for us, it seemed that there could be no choice more idyllic than Prince Edward Island. (And for the record, it was everything we expected and much, much more!) When we discover our "place," we seek an experience of home, a welcoming atmosphere and perhaps something beyond anything we have encountered before. It is a hotel situated in a national park, overlooking the sandy shores of the Atlantic Ocean, and all of this is remarkable. However, what truly makes it a "place" is how we were treated. From the moment we entered this historic hotel until the day we checked out, the entire establishment and its staff were dedicated to providing a level of service and hospitality we had never experienced before. We would walk through the door, and we were attended to hand and foot—at no extra charge. Whatever we needed was provided: a towel, a coffee, a snack, immediate seating in a feast-provisioned dining room, warm conversation, tourist information and more. It was also a "place" for us due to the feeling it evoked. I hold a memory of my wife and me in a Victorian sitting room—velvet-embroidered plush chairs and loungers arranged by a crackling fire, gazing out through floor-to-ceiling windows at the crashing surf. Every few minutes, smartly dressed attendants and servers would come to stoke the fire and offer drinks and finger foods, and the calm and peace of those evenings, that feeling of being cared for, noticed, and served, has not faded even once in the last eight years. It's something you're paying for, and while it's related to customer service, it also embodies the idea of going above and beyond—something that is today called "unreasonable hospitality."

Following a recent Global Leadership Summit, an annual leadership conference held in Chicago, our church has been focusing on a speech and book that emerged from this summit, titled "Unreasonable Hospitality: The Remarkable Power of Giving People More Than They Expect."[9] I love this title and theme— it makes sense and is a powerful way to make individuals feel valued. I mention the book here because we can all transform ordinary transactions into extraordinary experiences. It's something we can all offer within this idea of "place." A business can embody that, but we are exploring something much deeper. Let's revisit three key points mentioned earlier that highlight "place" and encourage us to view individuals through the lens of love: how we treat people, how it might affect their feelings and how it offers the ordinary that has the potential to become extraordinary.

People are looking for a place; thematically, we discuss how "welcome," and "Dalvay-By-the-Sea" serves as a prime example of the notion of giving people far more than they expect. I hope someone shares this with the hotel staff (I did when we were there!). To connect this to a space we invite those in poverty into, we seek to provide a "place" that is equally warm, generous, loving and inclusive. The way of love is both the path and means of welcome, but it must extend beyond anything ever known before. It is not a soup kitchen: it is not merely a place to grab a meal or find temporary shelter from the cold— though that has value too—but it must be crafted to feel like a "home." A home for those who are truly homeless that inspires them toward "homeness," as coined by a friend of mine. I will elabourate on this more later in the book.

Thus, "place" becomes a refuge that invites individuals to return again and again amidst the swirl and chaos of a life marked by homelessness, food insecurity, scarce relationships, a lack of love and acceptance.

In the book, Evicted: Poverty and Profit in the American City, Matthew Desmond describes people who lack a safe place: "Poverty can pile on—living it often means steering through gnarled thickets of interconnected misfortunes and trying not to go crazy! There were moments of calm, but life on balance was facing one crisis after another!"[10] A "place" that embodies love is a space where people feel seen and valued, a place where they are treated well. For its members, it offers a gentle refuge—a warm, inviting space that feels like home amid the chaos. A "place" that reflects love is a space where individuals feel, deeply and healing-wise, a more genuine welcome than they've ever experienced. It becomes a reality for them, gradually building toward an authentic community that makes them part of something larger. When you truly feel part of something—a sense of belonging, valued for who you are—this space becomes a place of health, wholeness, and healing. And then the ordinary transforms into the extraordinary.

When engaging with someone in poverty, miracles occur when love is demonstrated through seeing and being seen. Recognizing individuals with love—our way of "finding our person"—takes place in a special space and naturally involves a community. We all desire and require community, yearning to find one we can genuinely call our own. There is power in belonging. The work we do in our café and related programs aims to foster community and restore dignity in people's lives. Our efforts with and for individuals must be rooted in dignity and respect, making name recognition essential. Having worked in this environment for over seven years, I often remember someone's name, even if they haven't been around in years. I say, "Hey, Denis, where have you been? We've missed you!" This surprises Denis because society often perceives marginalized individuals as part of a crowd, a type, a category or a number. They frequently go unnoticed. Part of what we aim to cultivate through "love is a place" and through community is a space where people can truly belong, turning the invisible into the visible. Previously, Denis had been invisible to most people —almost as if he wasn't there at all. Conversely, this new way of living allowed him to be seen as a person, someone of worth, with hopes, dreams and his own story. Once, we hosted a focus group with individuals experiencing poverty, to explore new ideas and methods for improving our efforts. We were moving to a different location and the transition could be difficult for a group that finds change upsetting, so we needed to hear from them. We approached this thoughtfully, with a bit of flair: a gourmet meal, some light conversation, then we moved on to more serious topics, asking how we could better support them in the community and what resources were most needed. We received some responses, answered a few questions, and then a quiet voice, tearful and broken in its reply—a man we knew somewhat, but not well, someone living on the streets. "I only need one thing, and it has been hard to find when it never should! I would love to find someone, anyone, who wants to have a conversation with someone like me!"

There is a difference between being part of something and being part of an authentic community. We all need community; we gather with others who share similar interests, affinities, and experiences. Communities exist in rotary clubs, bike gangs, sewing circles and on the street. We were never meant to live alone; to be emotionally healthy—even in the most basic ways—we need other people. However, true restoration and a reconciled restorative community are only found in Jesus. We don't just want a gathering of people looking for food, shelter or clothing (although it may certainly start that way). We desire a place where people can gain something they may never have had before or, in some cases, never even imagined.

Susan visits our café drop-in, seeking a listening ear and understanding. She is currently living on the streets with her two cats, still holding onto the small hope that a future with a place to live is possible. She is an artist, often struggling to stay afloat but usually managing with her pension. This is a familiar story among people who aren't always good at managing the details of their lives and navigating regulations. Likewise, Susan's pension funds have been suspended until she provides the missing documents. In the meantime, she faces the trauma of eviction and living without a home until everything is sorted out. She arrives in tears, wondering how she will survive and, over tea and a muffin, we introduce her to a volunteer who helps her with the paperwork and assists her in finding an affordable place to live. Here at the café drop-in, she says, "I have found friends, caring, and a community who becomes a home and a place to belong."

An authentic community is where we discover the missing piece of what it truly means to have someone invest enough in us to listen to our story and love us unconditionally. I say this because part of taking a significant, risky step into community with others involves authenticity. It encourages people to go beyond just visiting as they seek to find their "place"—a leap for many. This begins a movement toward trust where trust may not have existed in their relationships for a long time or ever, and leads to healing. When I think about community, restoration, food, clothing, soup and rent payments, I see these as pathways to something profound. It is biblically true—for one example, consider this passage from Acts 4 as a call for authentic community: "All the believers were one in heart and mind." (Acts 4:32, NIV) No one claimed that any of their possessions was their own, but they shared everything they had (recognizing each other's practical and life needs). With great power, the Apostles continued to testify to the resurrection of the Lord Jesus, (the basis of authentic community in God's redemptive story.) God's grace was so powerfully at work in them all that there were no needy persons among them (reflecting spiritual flourishing). (vv. 32-34, NIV). Additions in text are my paraphrases.

The entire focus of a theological view on poverty alleviation centres on restoration, redemption and connectedness, and how these elements exist within community. Some colleagues and I conducted extensive research on this topic. A valuable perspective comes from the Chalmers Centre, which states: "We believe in a different approach to poverty—one that is rooted in God's redemptive story, the local church and transformational development." Sadly, many of the common ways of helping the poor don't reflect God's design for human flourishing. These approaches often trap people in the cycle of poverty and foster unhealthy dependency on others. This lack of transformation leaves followers of Jesus feeling stuck, frustrated, and exhausted. The essence of the way of love in community is about creating a space to gather around the table in pursuit of redemption and growth—essentially, giving a purpose to those who have never experienced one, and love to those who believed they could only be unlovable. In the way of love, there is more: a calling awaits!

Chapter Four

The Way of Love

I was touched by the following words on the power of love from a recent work of fiction by Alexander McCall Smith titled The Great Hippopotamus Hotel:

"She thought of love, for which there probably should be no limits. You could allow yourself to love with all your heart because that was always the right thing to do, in whatever circumstances. There were people who warned you that you had to protect yourself from the hurt that might come from loving too readily, but[...]she did not think they were right. You loved those with whom you shared the world, those whom you encountered on your way through life-you loved them with all your heart, freely and generously, and you should not worry about holding back, because the time we have is not a lengthy one and is over before we know it!"[11]

In a journey of love on behalf of the poor, which has carried us from "why" (overcoming objections) to "what" (a place and a community) and now to "how," we consider the way of love—the calling that draws us. How should we view such love? Love is not simply what we do after the task list is complete; it is not what we engage in at the end of things when we are not tired or have the time. Love is what we do before all else, who we are and who and what we must become! It is not about how we do things: it is the essence of the matter. So, friends, before we continue, let's take a moment to reflect on ourselves in the mirror. Drawing on an idea tied to prayer and contemplation, it is an examen, or sober evaluation of ourselves. Have we drifted from our abiding in Jesus, our first and primary love and our love for our neighbours? Do we truly love our brothers and sisters whom God places in our path and in our sphere of influence and impact? The Book of Revelation admonishes, "Yet I hold this against you: You have forsaken the love you had at first. Consider how far you have fallen! Repent and do the things you did at first. If you do not repent, I will come to you and remove your lampstand from its place" (2:4-5, NIV).

The way of love requires remembering, reflecting and participating; in this vital work, the most important thing is love! The way of love involves a place and a community. It also includes a call upon a person's heart (your heart) to do good. William Whiting Borden (1887–1913) was an American philanthropist and millionaire who became a missionary, dying in Egypt before reaching his chosen field, Gansu Province in China. He was born into a prominent and wealthy Illinois family, where his father made a fortune in silver mining. After his mother converted to Christianity in 1894, she took Borden to Chicago Avenue Church, later Moody Church, where he responded to the gospel preaching of the famed pulpiteer R.A. Torrey. From that point on, prayer and Bible study became the hallmarks of his life. Later, while travelling to London (once again under the preaching of Torrey, who was holding meetings there), Borden surrendered his life (to the displeasure of his father) to Christian service.

Using his own funds, he financed a rescue mission and provided personal service himself. One well-travelled English visitor, when asked what impressed him most about America, is said to have replied, "The sight of that young millionaire kneeling with his arms around a "bum" in the Yale hope mission." While Borden was studying at Princeton Theological Seminary—before his graduation, a professor (Charles R. Erdman) had this to say about him: "His judgment was so unerring and so mature that I always forgot there was such a difference in our ages. His complete consecration and devotion to Christ were a revelation to me, and his confidence in prayer a continual inspiration."

Borden intended to become a missionary in China, but he first decided to do some language studies in Cairo, where (in March 1913) he contracted cerebral meningitis and died within three weeks. On his grave was inscribed (suggested by Charles Erdman), "Apart from faith in Christ, there is no explanation for such a life." While the Bible was never found, it was reported that his mother found in his Bible the words "No Reserve" and a date suggesting they had been written shortly after he had renounced his fortune in favour of missions. Later, he was said to have written "No Retreat" after his father supposedly told him that, if he left for the mission field, he would never hold a position in the family business. Finally, shortly before he died in Egypt, he is supposed to have added the phrase "No Regrets."[12]

There is a call and a cost in the Christian life that demands sacrifice and commitment from us. You may not go to the mission field, train to be a Christian worker or pastor or find yourself in precarious circumstances due to the challenging service you provide, but you are called, and that calling becomes the way of love for others. I love this story because the call to the Christian life, along with the service and sacrifice it entails, prepares us for eternity and embodies the beauty of being swept up in an adventure and a need that transcends ourselves. Consider the adventure you could be swept into, the joy you could bring your King, the difference you could make! Numerous stories exist in a world that aches to be loved and shown a better way. The way of love is an adventure and demands a God-emanating call. The fact is, we can hear words so frequently that they become cliché and lose their relevance and meaning. "Call" can become one of those words. We understand the value of being called and urged by God toward something, but a fair question remains: how do we discover that?

In a call toward loving, investing in and caring for the poor, we consider nine aspects grouped into threes.

Call is defined by three paths:

Path 1	Understanding
Path 2	God's voice
Path 3	How God motivates us

Call is defined by three aims:

Aim 1	True relationship
Aim 2	Spiritual conversations
Aim 3	A better ending

Call is defined by three ways to walk:

Way 1	Walk in the way of being together in compassion
Way 2	Walk in the way of inviting people to dream
Way 3	Walk in the way of Holy Ground

In building a restorative and redemptive community, we will weave the aims and the ways to walk in the chapters to come. Here, we will establish the foundation for our examination of call through three paths:

Understanding

I have heard hundreds of stories and share some in this book; however, that merely reflects a fraction of all the stories I have encountered. The Book of Numbers revolves around counting, censuses, and communities. We need numbers—it is essential to count things and keep track, but it is equally important to explain what those numbers signify through stories. Numbers begins like this: "The Lord spoke to Moses in the tent of meeting in the Desert of Sinai on the first day of the census of the whole Israelite community by their clans and families, listing every man by name, one by one. You and Aaron are to count according to their divisions all the men in Israel who are twenty years old or more and able to serve in the army. One man from each tribe, each of them the head of his family, is to help you" (1:1-4, NIV).

Do you see what we have here? Numbers, a count is about to take place, but also stories, families, history, people. In our café work, we serve many individuals and maintain a prominent, consistent community, numbering in the hundreds. While we keep track of those statistics, we capture the stories. My staff, wife and family often tease me because I collect or invent phrases, slogans or sayings—I have many! One I coined in this focus on story is, "Everything we do rises and falls on stories." I mention story here in this section on the first three aspects of "call" because path one is understanding, and understanding arises to the extent that we are open and ready to hear people's stories. I have developed the principle that we can only invest in another person's life as much as we understand them. Please know that there is a distinction here: understanding is not the same as identification. I have never been homeless, I have never been addicted to drugs, and I have never known what it is to be evicted and have my meagre belongings thrown out onto a sidewalk. So, I cannot identify, but I can try to understand. Love and the ability to engage find their focus in understanding. Your initiative and boldness will determine how deeply you delve into this.

I was impressed by Mike Yankoski's book, Under the Overpass, in which he set out with only a backpack, sleeping bag and guitar, alongside his friend Sam. They aimed to understand what it was like to experience life on the streets of America, from Washington, DC to San Diego, without any money—sleeping in doorways and shelters and scavenging for food. It was not a matter of true identification but rather a quest for understanding. Here's the basis: Mike Yankoski is listening to a Sunday sermon in his church when he realizes he is not being the type of Christian he should be. Determined to change that, he devises a plan to help those in need on the streets. Sam Purvis, another Christian, joins him to live on the streets for the next five months—completely homeless and sometimes without food. Throughout their experiences, both discovered that their faith in God deepened as they sought to love and understand. Mike and Sam encountered numerous homeless individuals, many of whom struggled with drug or alcohol addiction and remained on the streets; however, there were others they got to know, providing Mike and Sam with a unique opportunity to assist those they had previously turned away from while navigating their middle-class lives. Through these encounters, Mike and Sam formed friendships and gained insights into surviving in a world where some churches have pushed the oppressed and marginalized aside. One thing neither of them anticipated was developing a deeper understanding of individuals struggling to survive without a home, dressed in worn clothes yet possessing a strong will to persevere.[13] What the author heard in church one Sunday reflects the experiences of countless others seated in worship centre chairs during or after a message delivered in our expansive church in Calgary, Alberta: the voice of God encouraging a response.

Through the Voice of God

Obviously, I don't know your experience; there are different takes and perspectives on what people believe regarding how and to what extent God speaks. Does He actually? Can we really hear Him? Is it possible to have that kind of relationship and intimacy with the God of the universe? Let's examine this question in two ways, because this is a critical path to a calling: to hear how God would want us to partner with Him. Scripture depicts God's will and voice as being heard and understood by

1. *Dreams and Visions:* God communicates through dreams and visions, which, when interpreted, can be viewed as divine messages and guidance. For instance, Jacob's ladder, the dreams of Joseph, the dreams of Pharaoh, Solomon's dream of wisdom and the dream from Pilate's wife.

2. *The word of God itself:* the Bible is the inerrant word of God and the primary source of guidance and communication. Hebrews 4:12 says, "For the word of God is alive and active.

Sharper than any double-edged sword, it penetrates even to dividing soul and spirit, joints and marrow; it judges the thoughts and attitudes of the heart" (NIV).

3. *Circumstances:* God communicates through the events and situations that occur in a person's life, using them to reveal His will or provide direction. For instance, Exodus 3: "Now Moses was tending the flock ... and he led the flock to the far side of the wilderness and came to Horeb, the mountain of God. There, the angel of the Lord appeared to him in flames of fire from within a bush[...]When the Lord saw that Moses had gone over to look, God called to him from within the bush, "Moses! Moses!" And Moses said, "Here I am." "Do not come any closer," God said. "Take off your sandals, for the place where you are standing is Holy Ground" (vv. 1,2,4, NIV).

4. *The Holy Spirit:* the Spirit serves as a guide and communicator, leading believers into truth and helping them understand God's will. For instance, in 1 Kings 19, we read about the gentle internal promptings of the "still small voice." "The Lord says to Elijah, 'Go out and stand on the mountain in the presence of the Lord, for the Lord is about to pass by.' Then a great and powerful wind tore the mountains apart and shattered the rocks before the Lord, but the Lord was not in the wind. After the wind, there was an earthquake, but the Lord was not in the

earthquake. After the earthquake came a fire, but the Lord was not in the fire. And after the fire came a gentle whisper" (vv. 11-12, NIV).

5. Angels—Messengers of God, sent to deliver messages or provide protection (Matthew 8:29; Luke 2:13; Luke 8:28-31; Hebrews 1:14).

6. *Wise Counsel*: Seeking and listening to wise counsel from others can also be a way God communicates, as it can provide guidance and perspective. "Let the wise listen and add to their learning, and let the discerning get guidance" (Proverbs 1:5, NIV).

7. *Creation:* Seen as a reflection of God's character and a way to understand His power and wisdom. "The Heavens declare the glory of God; the skies proclaim the work of His hands" (Psalm 19:1, NIV). "For since the creation of the world God's invisible qualities, His eternal power and divine nature, have been clearly seen, being understood from what has been made, so that people are without excuse" (Romans 1:20, NIV).

Secondly, God's voice is heard in our lives and hearts if we choose to listen. It can encompass everything mentioned above and can manifest as that still, small voice, that gentle whisper. Writing (just like God's Word) is also living and active. I finished some writing before work, went to the church, and a young man wandered in for a spontaneous meeting. He was in distress and had been sitting at a coffee shop, wondering what he should do and where he should go for help. A Jesus follower, he said to me, 'I never put much stock in this hearing the voice of God kind of thing, in fact I don't know if I ever really heard from God ever before. But as I was sitting there, I felt I should just be quiet and listen. And I heard this quiet voice tell me to come to the church, that they would help me.' I love this idea of just taking time to listen. Like any relationship with any level of intimacy, conversation, speaking, and listening is key. There is a fear that many have about things they would consider mystical, and for some, the idea of God actually being in a relationship with us where we can hear His voice is not so much that it is strange or weird, but rather that it is so incredible that we find it hard to believe God would do this for us. There are some steps we can follow, and by doing so, God's voice becomes clearer. We gain a sense of what God is saying to us and what He wants us to do about it:

1. Lean into God and draw close to Him.

2. Serve together in community and discern with others what God may be saying.

3. Take time apart to reflect, pray, and pause. Simply ask, "God, are you saying something to me?"

4. When you feel that God is asking something of you, do it! This might be experimental at first; it is a practice of discerning what you heard. Was it God? Was it my voice? Obey what you feel

He may be saying and see what happens with that. Over time, it becomes natural.

5. Spend as much time as possible studying and reading God's Word and in prayer. This is the best context for hearing, listening and aligning with His instructions and encouragements.

How God Uses Me

Focusing on gifts and talents, strengths, and desires is crucial to discerning how God will use us: where we serve, whom we serve and how that service will change, develop and grow within us. I briefly mentioned this earlier, but discerning our calling and considering service is as much about us as it is about those we serve. What I mean is, if we are deep and self-aware enough to understand our own stories and weaknesses—where we have grown and where we have healed—and come to build community with others from a place of strength, we will have much to offer. However, we also need to be reflective enough to recognize what we genuinely need from others in relationships.

I started this work from a place of brokenness, personal loss and devastation, but also with a sense of hope. I believe that this was my strength. There is an old, true adage that broken people love and serve broken people. While that is often true, it is not ideal. At one point in my vocation, I led a homeless shelter and managed 150 staff members. If even some of them had been truly broken, it could have led to disaster, and I have seen similar issues that might have caused catastrophes. We don't need to have everything together, and we are and will be imperfect, but we must approach the work with a toolbox of at least some key strengths. From this perspective, we can see the strengths and potential in those we serve, which in turn further strengthens us.

What It Means to Love

The extent to which we perceive, and experience grace and mercy shapes our understanding of their necessity within ourselves. Mercy involves recognizing my identity in God's eyes and acknowledging my need for grace just as much as those I serve. Let's return to our idea of rescue as we revisit the story of the Endurance. The crew of the Endurance found themselves in a state of crisis. The ship was crushed by the ice and sinking;

"The men rushed to safety on the ice, exhausted from their 3-day struggle to save the ship. They quickly set up their tents and fell into them. Just as they had dropped off to sleep, a crack in the ice tore through their camp and they had to scramble to another spot for safety. It was suddenly clear they were going to face an extraordinary challenge just to stay alive. The men had expected to be working in relative comfort in base camp or to be doing ship's work. Instead, they were stranded on a vast, unstable layer of ice that was their only refuge from the depths of the Weddell Sea, or, even worse, the jaws of a killer whale or sea leopard. And it was -16 degrees Fahrenheit."[14]

We started this book talking about the fears and objections to why you should or shouldn't serve the poor. Recall the guy at your back fence and you just don't want to be dealing with that, or, as I saw today, a group of custodians having to try to move on a drug-addicted individual out of a bathroom. Probably all these workers wanted was a hot cup of coffee and a donut. We journeyed from there and we began to look at the person not the problem. We have spent a lot of time-sharing principles on care and call, no matter who you may be called to love and serve, as long as it is somebody. The above description of the Endurance is both about them and about us.

Those We Serve

They are like the ones stranded on the ice, thinking things would have been different, maybe just a little more comfortable. Surrounded by ice, snow and cold, they endure the darkest nights they have ever known. Encampments and tents, just trying to get a bit of sleep, but far too exhausted for it, then making the necessary move to another spot, to another place, with no more comfort than they knew in the last one and quite possibly much less. As in the description, these are eking out an existence that is an "extraordinary challenge just to stay alive." This is their story, and the stories of those in the food line, at the tables and rustling through the musty clothing. The ones grumbling in the bread rack line and the bigger, more boisterous ones pushing ahead for the desserts. And these are the ones when the service and program close after dinner, when the coffee urns are dry, and the mops and buckets come out, as rain falls or snow scatters and the mercury drops. They pack up their small belongings, carefully rewrapped and packed 1.000 times—and they hesitate, lingering for a glass of water, a bathroom break and a small unrequited wish: to go to a cozy house, crawl under a down comforter and listen to the startup and shutdown of a central furnace.

Those Who Serve

This is us: asking the question while feeling so fearful about it at the same time. Our life circumstances are probably quite different, yet we are still on the ice. Maybe we are that group who simply listened to a sermon and thought we should do something about it (guilted as we were), and now we find ourselves here, unsure why and uncertain of what to expect. We enjoy our comfort; we aren't great at long, drawn-out needy conversations, and we don't know what to say. It feels like being on ice, lacking any sense of rhythm in a conversation across a table, feeling awkward. We aren't struggling to stay alive here; this isn't life and death, but it could be as uncomfortable as you have ever felt. Perhaps your scramble onto this ice is a way to find a renewed sense of closeness to God. You have felt tired for a long time. You pray, and it echoes empty; you read Scripture, and it feels old. As one song says, even your Hallelujah is tired. Your experience cannot be the same as theirs, but you know you must try. It is critical that you love, and what if these people are your people? What if this is the very thing? What if?

The way of love guides us away from problems, pain, complications, questions and objections toward people or a person. It encompasses a place, a community and a call to a person's heart (your heart) to do good. Friends—fellow called ones—this is the way of love. A place to belong, a community to belong to, a call on our hearts for understanding, the voice of God, and being used by God. Your person is waiting at the table!

Chapter Five

The Right Kind of Welcome

In an earlier chapter, we described a friendship that we will revisit here: the relationship between Jesus, Mary, Martha and Lazarus. More than friends to Jesus, they (and their home) served as a refuge for Him. He loved them deeply and consistently; in their company, He found rest, understanding and devotion. During one of His visits with them, a question of sorts arose: "What is the one necessary thing?" We pick up the story—

"As Jesus and His disciples were on their way, He came to a village where a woman named Martha opened her home to Him. She had a sister named Mary, who sat at the Lord's feet, listening to what He said. But Martha was distracted by all the preparations that had to be made. She came to Him and asked, 'Lord, don't you care that my sister has left me to do the work by myself? Tell her to help me!' 'Martha, Martha,' the Lord answered, 'You are worried and upset about many things, but few things are needed— or indeed only one. Mary has chosen what is better, and it will not be taken away from her'" (Luke 10:38-42, NIV).

Regarding the Scripture above, Henri Nouwen, a profound thinker and teacher of contemplative spiritual life, said, "Jesus' response to our worry-filled lives is quite different. He asks us to shift our point of focus, to move the centre of our attention, and to change our priorities. Jesus wants us to move from the 'many things' to the 'one necessary thing.'" We need to recognize that Jesus, in no way, wants us to abandon our multifaceted worlds. Instead, He desires that we live within them while remaining firmly rooted at the centre of all things. Jesus does not speak about a change in activities, contacts, or pace. He talks about a change of heart. This change of heart makes everything different, even while everything appears to remain the same. This is the meaning of the Scripture verse, "But seek his kingdom, and these things will be given to you" (Luke 12:31, NIV). What matters is where our hearts are. When we worry, we have our hearts in the wrong place. Jesus asks us to move our hearts to the centre, where all other things fall into place.

I love this picture; I go back to it again and again. During the flurry of life—deadlines, bills, disappointments and complications, like a ship tossed at sea, a tempest raging, a great struggle to right itself, to right yourself—there is a place. In our Scripture, Mary finds the one thing that is necessary in the shipwreck of life: to sit at Jesus' feet; to stop, to listen, to breathe. Sometimes we are forced to slow it down. I recall sitting at the feet of Jesus for two weeks in 2021, recovering from a health scare and taking time to reflect and find refuge.

In the Old Testament, there is a powerful declaration of trust in God's protection and His provision for everything, emphasizing that those who make God their refuge will always find safety under His care. No matter who we are or what we have experienced, it is vital that we feel safe and secure, for there is a promise that we will be delivered from danger, and that God is an unwavering and reliable presence in times of trouble. Recently, I have been moved by the image of refuge described in Psalm 91: "Whoever dwells in the shelter of the Highest will rest in the shadow of the Almighty. I will say of the Lord, 'He is my refuge and my fortress, my God in whom I trust'" (vv. 1-2, NIV).

I believe I still have it—a painting that used to hang in my home office. It's the kind of painting that slows everything down for me. We need that, don't we? To stop long enough, to breathe deeply, to get off the relentless wheel of time and realize that the way to a united heart and soul is in Him. What He desires to do in others through us becomes our healing, moment by moment, as we find our home in Jesus. The picture ministers to me; it brings peace and calm. It depicts a wood, overflowing with trees, the greenest of greens, with leaves carpeting the brown, moist earth. I can close my eyes and imagine its softness, the sound of a slow and healing walk. There are birds; with good reason, the artist didn't choose ravens or hawks, but blue songbirds seem to weave and flit among the branches. The path I am on is wide, resplendent, and peaceful, but ahead and to the right is a mailbox (I have always wondered and imagined what message might lie within: what letter, what card, what surprise). Then there's another path, which, while more shaded, seems to have less sun.

Still, this path appears to have a calling, a drawing; it seems shorter and narrower, but it winds around a bend, disappearing, and I have always wondered about that path. I have no idea what the artist of that painting was suggesting, but it does remind me of a road less travelled (as one writer put it), and makes me wonder, which is the path that makes all the difference?

In Chapter 4, we began to explore the concept of call, dedicating considerable time to it because call serves as the essential path through the woods that leads us to the feet of Jesus and prepares both us and others for an inner place we have long overlooked. We stated that in a call toward loving, investing in and caring for the poor, we consider nine principles grouped in threes. In the last chapter, we examined: the path of understanding, the path of the voice of God (how He speaks to us) and the path of how God uses us (what God might be saying about how He wants to use you). In this chapter, we explore three principles of loving, caring and investing, framed by three aims: fostering relationships, engaging in spiritual conversations and achieving better endings.

Let's delve deeper into the story of a group of friends: Jesus and the sisters Mary and Martha. "As Jesus and the disciples were on their way, he came to a village where a woman named Martha opened her home to him. She had a sister called Mary, who sat at the Lord's feet listening to what he said" (Luke 10:38-39, NIV). The first relationship this addresses is the concept of welcome. This is a word that can easily be overlooked, taken for granted or dismissed, leading to a missed opportunity to recognize the important role of hospitality. But I want us to pause and reflect deeply on what it means to welcome people—not only into a space we might invite them into, such as a church, home or business—but also into our hearts.

In the Gospels, Jesus frequently engages in ministry through healing, teaching and blessing. In Luke 10, He actively teaches, preaches and corrects while launching a movement of 72 disciples, sending them out and welcoming them back. He shares the story of the Good Samaritan and journeys across a broad area as these events unfold. He is also skilled at intentionally practicing rest and rejuvenation, often setting aside time to pray, spending time alone in communion with God and simply enjoying moments of solitude. From His activities, Jesus and some disciples arrive in Bethany, a village on the eastern slopes of the Mount of Olives and the home of Martha and Mary. They are welcomed into this home that Jesus knows well. This is one example of a time set apart to rest and enjoy friendship, but I want you to notice something very particular here. The Scripture notes that as they come to the door of this home, they are greeted by Martha. You are familiar with this story, and what you might not have noticed is that the Scripture here describes two different kinds of welcome. How we welcome reflects our purpose and intent, essentially comprising three elements: how we love, how we consider personal space (our home, our time, our comforts) and how flexible our idea of family is.

While it is true that some aspects of this are based on personality and perhaps even upbringing, we are predominantly discussing a healed and whole heart, connected to welcome. I grew up hearing the repeated stories of my paternal grandmother's concept of welcome. She truly was one of the kindest people I have ever known, and I experienced the warmth and embrace of that kindness from childhood into adulthood. The stories my father tells recount not knowing, night to night, where he would be sleeping. Many individuals facing a need or challenging situation would receive a nourishing meal and a place to sleep. During a recent visit, he shared a story about a woman who looked threadbare and forlorn, dragging a suitcase down the sidewalk past the front window of their house. Out would go my grandmother, carefully taking the woman's arm and steering her to the hearth and home.

To make a brief psychological aside here, it might be helpful to remind ourselves of the concept and types of space. An anthropologist by the name of Edward T. Hall identified four zones that describe different degrees of personal space and comfort:[15]

Zones of Personal Space and Comfort

Intimate: You are essentially 0-45cm away from someone. These individuals are emotionally close to us, including family members, partners and, in my personal space and that of my wife's, our dogs. This signifies a welcome of caring and involves emotional moments where we share a hug or a kiss and provide support to each other.

Personal: You are about 45cm to 1.2m away from someone. These are individuals you are close to but not as near as in the intimate zone; they could be friends or colleagues. They may include people present with you in meetings or workshops, engaging in casual conversations at meals, or participating in social activities, among others. I would suggest this as what I am calling a second kind of welcome.

Social: You are 1.2–3.6m apart. (These, of course, are approximations). These tend to be more formal or impersonal connections, such as colleagues or professionals, during outdoor activities, large meetings and other similar settings.

Public: You are 3.6m and beyond. Almost any member of the public, at almost any time, falls into this dynamic.

I share these as a reminder of these zones that are reasonable and appropriate depending on the relationship, but also to consider whether the zones can and should be crossed based on how God is prompting us to think about welcome.

In my research, I encountered several experiments for people to consider what it means to move into the intimate zone. One exercise involves you and a partner, standing facing each other at opposite ends of the room. Now, begin to speak to your partner while walking very slowly toward them. Continue the conversation as you gradually move closer. Try to observe your feelings throughout this process. Continue moving toward each other until only a few centimetres remain between you—the intimate zone. Take a moment to discuss your feelings and thoughts during this exercise.

Now, let's return to Luke 10 and the two kinds of welcome I am suggesting. Again, it is Martha at the door greeting Jesus and the disciples. Martha is the hostess with the mostest. (I once heard a preacher ask whether Martha Stewart—the pop culture billionaire hostess—might have been named after her.) Her welcome is genuinely warm and hospitable; she certainly aims to make Jesus feel comfortable in her home, encouraging Him to sit down and put His feet up while she serves a glass of sweet red wine (I don't think a Nespresso was an option just yet). While He relaxes, she gets busy preparing the rare roast beast. "Martha became exasperated by finishing the numerous household chores in preparation for her guests" (Luke 10:40, NIV). Martha's level of welcome is a "personal zone" kind of welcome. It's not intimate; it's friendship. It's about doing for another. There is no question that a close relationship exists between Martha and Jesus, but it's a more practical, deeds-oriented kind of welcome than what we see with Mary. Continuing in Luke 10, we encounter a second kind of welcome. Mary is at the "intimate zone" with Jesus, a place not merely of friendship or closeness, but of genuine intimacy, reflecting the depth of the mutual relationship between Jesus and Mary—a welcome of the heart. How does Mary welcome Jesus? She embraces Him as someone who perceives her heart, while responding as one who yearns to understand His heart. The essence of a true and profound relationship is to discover and flourish within a community where each person is accepted for who they are. It embodies a deeper vision, an authentic community that serves as a rescue operation for those on the margins—a rescue of the heart. To see people as if they have never been seen before, to forge relationships as if they have never experienced a meaningful one, or any relationship at all. Mary's welcome consists of sitting at the Master's feet, undistracted.

The second aim of the call to love, care, and invest in those living on the margins is to discover how God is both motivating and changing us, particularly through spiritual conversations. Henri Nouwen also said this: "I was constantly bothered by all the interruptions to my day of work in ministry until I realized that the interruptions are the ministry."[16] I love this! Jesus, of course, experienced frequent interruptions, and within these interruptions was found the very centre of His healing, love, and compassion. The point is, in this work, we must embrace interruptions or slow things down enough to hear what God is revealing about our own preconceived ideas as we engage with others for the long haul. This is the place of calling—to see the people in front of you not as your interruptions but as your ministry.

My entire ministry life revolves around interruptions! I mentioned interruptions earlier because, as we pursue intimacy or a close, caring friendship or relationship with anyone we seek to love and invest in, we need to be attentive to what God is doing. Therefore, God also interrupts and calls us to slow down, be still, listen, learn and love. We realize that, by slowing down, we not only hear what is happening with someone else but also how God uses others to help us understand our circumstances. As C.S. Lewis says, "The great thing, if one can, is to stop regarding all the unpleasant things as interruptions of one's 'own' or 'real' life. The truth is of course that what one calls the interruptions are precisely one's real life—the life God is sending one day by day."[17]

As I mentioned, writing is a living and active process. In the room where I was working the other morning, there was a loud knock on the door. A woman was frantically looking for my assistant to help her and her husband unload a truck filled with bags of used clothes that they were donating. I explained that my assistant would not be in until later, and somewhere in the recesses of my brain, I felt the urge to suggest she come back. However, a larger heart prevailed. I cheerfully offered to assist them, and we unloaded all the bags. As we finished, she looked at me and said, "I know you. You prayed for me and my two friends when we were in a difficult place after church one morning; it meant so much!" I told her that I did remember that occasion, and suddenly she grabbed my hands and said, "Pray for me. I am travelling to Europe, and I would appreciate your prayers. I know that God arranged this for today." And so, we prayed, and I returned to my office, knowing that in the face of this, any other work could wait.

I want to emphasize the value of pausing for a spiritual conversation, or perhaps a better phrase would be spiritual presence. We are there for people, and in our busy lives, this may come as an interruption to a hectic day or a series of tasks. Alternatively, it may feel like an unrelenting call to come forward and hear God in another. I assume that Martha likely wasn't fond of interruptions. There's a roast in the oven, potatoes to peel, and a carpet to vacuum (or whatever the equivalent tasks were in Bethany). I don't get the impression that the contemplative life was her strength. To be fair to her, there is value in what she was doing. When we host guests for the weekend, the to-do list emerges: change the sheets, vacuum the sofas and carpets, take out the recyclables and do the dusting. It wouldn't be the warmest reception if I told my wife, "Sorry, I am just sitting at the feet of Jesus, you are on your own!"

And yet, regardless of our schedule, the most important thing is to be present for our guests and to make them feel welcome. A well-meaning congregant once remarked that Mary was lazy. However, Mary understood when to listen, remain quiet and engage wholeheartedly in prayer and worship. I cherish the freedom this brings us, both for ourselves and for others. She absorbed every Word Jesus spoke. He had something for her—this was her time. Jesus has something for you, too; this may be your time to sit at His feet—to hear, to be with another, to listen. We often underestimate the importance of practicing His presence! Being present in ministry not only benefits those we serve but also enriches us. "Be still and know that I am God; I will be exalted among the nations, I will be exalted in the earth" (Psalms 46:10, NIV).

The third aim in the call to love, care for and invest in those who are in poverty, broken and searching to discover how God motivates and changes us is through better endings. Anyone who knows me understands that I love Christmas! My kids sometimes say that, for me, everything revolves around celebration. I cherish, most of all, the Advent and Christmas story—the coming of Jesus, the long-awaited time when the weary world rejoices! I also appreciate the warmth and vibrancy of it all: the carols, the ringing of bells, the glow of lights, the hope and the feeling that people pay a bit more attention to others while focusing a little less on their own agendas. I believe that what powerfully impacts me is the sense of light coming into the world and the story; the better ending prophesied (a story foretold) that would one day come. "For to us a child is born, to us a son is given, and the government will be on His shoulders. And He will be called Wonderful Counsellor, Mighty God, Everlasting Father, Prince of Peace" (Isaiah 9:6, NIV). When I think of our café and the people there—gathered around tables, searching for clothing, in the meal line, listening to songs of worship—I wonder if the love being sung around them, shared by joyful volunteers, and the laughter among their community of new and hoped-for friends could truly be part of something new for them. I think of Christmas and the concepts of peace and hope, and I contemplate what God is building, like a "candle in a window." I have heard of a similar notion before, and then one night, while we hosted a celebration in our community, featuring a roast beef dinner and an avalanche of sugar, I looked out the window and saw lights reflecting. I imagined what it would be like for people whose lives were in tatters, gazing through our large windows and seeing people filled with so much joy. I wondered if they might peer through those windows and see a glimmer of hope, like a candle in a window, and realize that they, too, could have it.

This "candle in a window" is also part of American history. In the United States, during colonial times, the sight of a lit candle in a window at Christmas signified that a building or home was open and welcoming to those passing by, and that shelter and food would be available. Furthermore, this practice traces back to Irish Catholics during a time of oppression, when families displayed candles at Christmas to let priests know that the home of light was a haven during persecution.[18] It was the idea and theme of a church providing a space that was open and welcoming to those passing by, where food and community were available. It would be a place where we could invite both those searching for a sense of belonging and those feeling called to be a part of a community where, because of Jesus, we all walk as one, with no walls, barriers, or discrimination.

A final look (for this chapter) at Luke 10:

"But Martha was distracted by all the preparations that had to be made. She came to him and asked, 'Lord, don't you care that my sister has left me to do the work by myself? Tell her to help me!' 'Martha, Martha,' the Lord answered, 'you are worried and upset by many things, but few things are needed-or indeed only one. Mary has chosen what is better, and it will not be taken away from her" (vv. 40-41, NIV).

Earlier, I spoke about the two different kinds of welcome and asked you to consider how far-reaching your idea of family is. I believe it was very flexible indeed for my grandmother and the woman with the rolling suitcase!

Every week, our staff and I have people come and express that the space God provides feels like home to them, and that we are their family. In earlier days, I wondered if that was merely something they said, but I now know it to be true. In these chapters, I have been riffing on "call" because the idea of motivation comes from the heart and never from what you think you should do. There is no personal agenda in it; the motivation arises from the brokenness of people and the agony of their lives seeking a place that grabs you and will not let you go. I leave you in this chapter with Troy, a dear friend who I believe is now with the Lord. He lost his mother on the east coast of Canada and found family at that time in an old, cracked and musty church basement. He found friends and, more importantly, family, not because they were volunteering, but because they loved. Their aim was true!

Chapter Six

The One Who Walks Beside

"Who is the third who walks always beside you?
When I count, there are only you and I together
But when I look ahead up the white road
There is always another one walking beside you
Gliding wrapt in a brown mantle, hooded
I do not know whether a man or a woman
But who is that on the other side of you?"
—TS Eliot "The Waste Land"[19]

I stroll with my wonderful wife along a winding path. It's spring, and the surroundings are brown: weeds and scorched grass, pressed buds on trees, and elements yearning to emerge. Our dog, a coonhound by breed, sniffs at all these new scents as the pathway winds by the valley and swiftly flowing waters. It feels fresh, clean and peaceful, and as we walk, holding hands, we see the beauty and we experience a calmness, a rest, as if Jesus is physically on this same road. This experience reminds me of another story in which two men were walking along a roadside when Jesus joined them.

"Now, that same day two of them were going to a village called Emmaus, about seven miles from Jerusalem. They were talking with each other about everything that had happened. As they talked and discussed these things with each other, Jesus himself came up and walked along with them; but they were kept from recognizing him. He asked them, "What are you discussing together as you walk along?" They stood still, their faces downcast. One of them, named Cleopas, asked him, "Are you the only one visiting Jerusalem who does not know the things that have happened there in these days?" "What things?" he asked. "About Jesus of Nazareth," they replied. "He was a prophet, powerful in word and deed before God and all the people. The chief priests and our rulers handed him over to be sentenced to death, and they crucified him; but we had hoped that he was the one who was going to redeem Israel. And what is more, it is the third day since all this took place. In addition, some of our women amazed us. They went to the tomb early this morning but didn't find his body. They came and told us that they had seen a vision of angels, who said he was alive. Then some of our companions went to the tomb and found it just as the women had said, but they did not see Jesus." He said to them, "How foolish you are, and how slow to believe all that the prophets have spoken! Did not the Messiah have to suffer these things and then enter his glory?" [...]So, he went in to stay with them. When he was at the table with them, he took bread, gave thanks, broke it and began to give it to them. Then their eyes were opened, and they recognized him, and he disappeared from their sight. They asked each other, "Were not our hearts burning within us while he talked with us on the road and opened the Scriptures to us" (Luke 24:13-32, NIV). The question I have for each of us, arising from this story that takes place on the day of Christ's resurrection, is, "What do you think can happen on a walk?" In my search for calm in my soul and my quest to find my inner self—to slow down and see, feel and experience God—I have explored many books, studies, and tutors. One such figure is the author and teacher Mark Buchanan, whose relatively recent book, God Walk: Moving at the Speed of Your Soul, has resonated with this journey. Buchanan says, "Jesus Himself does not choose the straightway. He wanders highways and byways. He seeks out lonely places. He rambles about in the wilderness. He plots the longest distance between two points and takes that. Given a choice between a safe quick route and a slow dangerous one, He almost always picks the latter."[20]

As we have considered "call", the foundation of this time together has been a deep reflection to discover what motivates your faith journey. Call it passion, call it compassion, call it gift, call it journey... yes, perhaps "journey" is the best word. I know this word is often used to describe various adventures, movements and brands, but it may be the most fitting, as it also suggests "path" and reflects the walk we are on. I truly get excited about the phrase "where we find ourselves!"

I believe this captures the essence of adventure— serving a God who draws us into something much larger and more magnificent than ourselves! It involves joining a movement or accepting a mission —a vibrant and exhilarating community experience—

yes, once again, bigger than yourself. I've been telling you about a café, something that started small with lukewarm coffee and day-old muffins and then grew into something more. The "bigger" I mentioned, in terms of people serving and being served, expanded from 20 to hundreds. It was a wave that I had the chance to ride. Have you ever felt that experience of riding the wave, joining Him in His ongoing work? With God, you embark on an adventure without knowing where it will lead.

In a previous book I authored, Stuk: Helping People Find a Better End to Their Stories, I also reflected on the idea of adventure in this calling to serve the poor and expressed it as follows:

"Perhaps you have had the privilege of spending time with, befriending, or feeling burdened over (as the Apostle James describes) 'orphans and widows in their distress'—the poor, addicted, lost, wandering, abused, lonely, isolated, hopeless, and hopeful all at once. The purpose God calls us to is to love people in the name of Jesus and guide them to a place far beyond where they are... and beyond what they ever dreamed they could become. The images we create with our eyes and hearts can be helpful; therefore, it may be truly beneficial to view this as a journey and a path we are walking along. Like the Gospel story of Jesus walking with some confused and disoriented souls on the road to Emmaus; they share what they don't understand, and He helps them make sense of it all, guiding them to discover a better way and to fully embrace a story they could only dream of but never attain. The journey we are on is to understand a story we are asked to be part of in the lives of orphans and widows, while learning lessons that have the potential to change lives forever! This call is for those who walk with, love, care for, are inspired by, and want to make a genuine and lasting difference in the lives of those facing these tough times. And here is our exciting and possibly life-changing encouragement for you: When we walk with people, we open a door to a potential opportunity (if they desire it and are willing to join us) to bring hope that lasts, perhaps for the very first time."[21]

God creates a world and gives it to us. In our hands, lie control and opportunity; we are handed the reins, which embody both beauty and love. This is his way —the way He loves, believes and trusts. When God grants us creation, hope, sky, trees and mountains, He also provides life and a playground for adventure. You can climb the highest peak, sail the deepest ocean, pen and sing a song, write the greatest novel or pick apples from a sprawling tree to make a juicy, mouthwatering apple pie. In all that He has given us, there are countless joys and endless discoveries— like pearls and treasures hidden in a field. The Bible also discusses this: "The kingdom of heaven is like treasure hidden in a field. When a man found it, he hid it again, and then in his joy went and sold all he had and bought that field" (Matthew 13:44, NIV). Envision the most stunning location you can conceive of—a place you've been to, a destination you yearn to revisit. It's a joyful space that is uniquely yours—your blessing from God. My wife and I took a trip down the picturesque Oregon coast for her 50th birthday. One evening, we turned into a park by the ocean, leaned back in the car holding hands, closed our eyes, heard the waves, and felt the breeze, a gift wrapping us like a blanket—a memory that stays with us as if it were in our DNA. And so, the world—this Earth, this gift to us—is an adventure, like that ocean breeze and the great sea beyond. There is something that is part of us, this call we have been discussing, to make a difference, to be swept into what lies beyond our wildest imaginings!

In the book, Love and War, John and Stasi Eldredge write,

"A good story has adventure to it. An unknown terrain explored. A wilderness survived. A mountain won. A destination reached. And the story of how it all unfolded -or unravelled—told over and over again. Sometimes risk is involved. Sometimes danger. Often deep beauty. Adventures can be had on our own or with a group. They can entail discovering a new city or acquiring a new talent. The right kind of adventures help us to become more the person we long to be."[22]

The right kind of adventure helps us better become the person we long to be. This is the very crux of the "call" we are drawn toward. Beginning in Chapter Four, we mentioned that in a call toward loving, investing in, and caring for the poor, we would consider nine principles grouped in threes.

In Chapter Four, we examined

1. The path of understanding

2. The path of the voice of God (how He speaks to us)

3. The path of how God uses us (what might God be saying about how He wants to use you).

In Chapter Five, we examined

1. The aim of the relationship (or, more specifically, the right kind of welcome)

2. The aim of spiritual conversations, which involves paying attention to how God communicates

3. The aim of better endings is to help individuals recognize qualities within themselves that they may not see.

In this chapter, we explore the theme of the journey we are on and how we walk alongside others:

1. To walk in the way of being together with others in their suffering

2. To walk in the way of inviting people into a life of dreams

3. To walk on Holy Ground.

Let's examine the three approaches we will use for these walks. However, it's crucial to recognize that neither we nor those we accompany are ever alone on this journey. I return us (once more) to the figure inspiring a recovery operation for the poor. While Sir Ernest does not write much about it, he was a man of faith, raised that way, and, as we ultimately discovered, it was a critical part of what he considered his basis for success. He wrote in his autobiography, South, that any retelling of the Endurance story would be "incomplete without a reference to a subject very near to our hearts." [23] He tried to articulate the spiritual dimension of his feelings:

"When I look back at those days, I have no doubt that Providence guided us, not only across the snow fields, but across the storm-white sea that separated Elephant Island from our landing place on South Georgia. I know that during that long and racking march of 36 hours over the unnamed mountains and glaciers of South Georgia, it seemed to me that we were four, not three. I said nothing to my companions on the point, but afterward Worsley said to me, 'Boss, I had a curious feeling on the march that there was another person with us.' Crean confessed to the same idea."[24]

So, in this "call"—as the one "very near to our hearts" leads us—what is the slow walk He is guiding us toward? The first critical dynamic we consider is that we do not walk alone, regardless of what we face— whether wasteland or summit. Walking in "the way of being together with others in their suffering" has two elements to it:

1. Being with someone during their suffering (and I have journeyed much with people living out a definition of compassion: "to suffer alongside") is truly a ministry of being present without judgment or perhaps even opinion.

2. Being with someone during their suffering means addressing practical needs before attending to spiritual ones (as the Bible calls it, a cup of cold water).

In examining the first element, Phil C. Zylla writes, "God is the author of compassion. Compassion involves 'suffering with' those who are in anguish and moving into the situations of the most afflicted with active help. This is the centre of a Christian theology of suffering. The movement of God into the world's brokenness and every situation of fear and oppression is the core Biblical message about who God is. God is love." [25]

In this book, we speak of a "ministry of presence" and the power of "being there." For people who are afflicted, grieving or isolated (all aspects of suffering), we have studied the importance of place and community. From this environment, we observe all the issues that lead to poverty, which in turn become the defining characteristics of suffering: addiction, abuse, lack of acceptance, mental illness, disabilities, purposelessness and hopelessness. This, by necessity, calls for a response, and that response is the "recovery operation" for the poor that we have been considering.

Thus, as we reflect on place, community and calling, we recognize that engagement with those who suffer must be characterized by

- The pursuit of relationships with one another and with God

- The belief that God is active in the life of someone who is suffering

- The belief that the story we are part of is one of hope and change

- The belief that prayer can unleash the power to break strongholds and set captives free (Luke 4; Isaiah 61)

- The belief that, as we gather at the table or walk with our friend along the road, there is an opportunity to tackle loneliness and isolation—overcoming shame

The second element is the "cup of cold water" as an expression of love in action. Here are two scriptures that illustrate this concept:

"What good is it, my brothers and sisters, if someone claims to have faith but has no deeds? Can such faith save them? Suppose a brother or a sister is without clothes and daily food. If one of you says to them, 'Go in peace; keep warm and well fed, ' but does nothing about their physical needs, what good is it? In the same way, faith by itself, if it is not accompanied by action, is dead" (James 2:14-17, NIV).

"And whoever gives even a cup of cold water to one of these little ones in the name of a disciple-truly I say to you, that person will not lose their reward" (Matthew 10:42, NIV).

These verses are part of a broader movement in ministry where Jesus sends out His disciples to preach and heal, emphasizing the importance of the message and the ministry, which includes how those ministering on His behalf will be received. What is wonderful about what Jesus teaches through various verses is that anyone who serves on His behalf is "for Him" and is to be welcomed and supported. It does not stretch the words or intent too far to say that God sees all and cares for all.

Earlier in this chapter, Jesus says, "Are not two sparrows sold for a penny? Yet not one of them will fall to the ground outside your father's care. And even the very hairs of your head are all numbered. So don't be afraid; you are worth more than many sparrows" (Matthew 10: 29-31, NIV). Therefore, there is assurance that those who serve those belonging to Him, even in the smallest acts, will be rewarded. We walk together in suffering to the extent that we share a journey of "being there" for others, removing walls, barriers and prejudices.

Elmer's Story

"Do you have five minutes, Pastor?" I know it's never

just five minutes. He has a story to share and perhaps a request to make, and he needs a listening ear. Not merely for conversation, but also to feel valued and acknowledged for what matters to him. Will I listen? I am busy, and my task list keeps growing, but I must pause and listen because there might not be anyone else in his life who will do the same. This requires an active, compassionate and engaged presence for listening. In church and pastoral care, we often talk about a ministry of presence, which means being fully present and engaged. Many acts of kindness can be seen as a cup of cold water, and this is one of them. Elmer shares a long, winding story full of heartbreak and hope, and I set aside my agenda to listen and pray, being there—being fully present! This shows how our calling is to walk alongside others in their suffering.

Another way to support others is by "walking in the way of inviting people into a life of dreams." The journey of inviting people into a life of dreams is a journey of "bare chests." Sounds strange, I know. The Book of Proverbs offers one of the most significant contexts in all of Scripture for both service and sacrifice in making a positive impact on the lives of the poor.

"Whoever is kind to the poor lends to the Lord, and he will reward them for what they have done." (Proverbs 19:17, NIV).

"If a king judges the poor with fairness, his throne will be established forever. (Proverbs 29:14, NIV).

"Whoever increases wealth by taking interest or profit from the poor amasses it for another, who will be kind to the poor." (Proverbs 28:8, NIV).

The sacrifice involved in serving the vulnerable, those on the margins and those in greatest need, is not made or extended to seek reward; instead, the result comes from this walk that proclaims, "Truly I tell you, whatever you did for one of the least of these brothers and sisters of mine, you did for me" (Matthew 25:40, NIV). Therefore, our sacrifice for others is a sacrifice for Jesus. Specifically, what kind of sacrifice is referenced? "For when you saw me hungry, you fed me. When you found me thirsty, you gave me something to drink. When I had no place to stay, you invited me in, and when I was poorly clothed, you covered me. When I was sick you tenderly cared for me, and when I was in prison you visited me" (Matthew 25: 35-36, NIV).

There is service and sacrifice that we undertake for others with Jesus, demonstrating to people that, beyond merely being present, we believe in who they are and who they can become. I have a staff member who does an exceptional job in our café, serving hot meals two or three times a week to hundreds of guests. She recently befriended a man (let's call him Carl). Carl struggles with addiction. If you saw him on the street (as in the story of the Good Samaritan and that uppity Levitical priest), you would avoid him. His hair is a knotted mess. His clothes are ragged, unkempt and dingy. The odor on him is a combination of alcohol, tobacco, and persistent bad breath. Once again, he shows up inebriated and spiraling into his addictions, needing to be escorted out once more. His family, friends and others are starting to write him off. But not my staff member; she says, "He will get there; we must believe in Him." It's a long road, but it's a journey he will undertake.

Turning to God completely and in surrender involves actions as well as a transformation of both heart and deed, not merely words. Scripture elsewhere mentions giving both shirt and coat (tunic); indeed, it suggests that if required, one might go "bare-chested" so that another has what they need. The connection that arises from this level of sacrifice not only reflects a change within our hearts but also, like cold water, serves as a gift that perhaps others have never known. This kind of love opens people to a life of dreams.

Our final way to walk—our final path in these "calls" to love the poor in a profoundly different way—requires a change in outlook, hope and life that is permanent and eternal. It represents an understanding of what we describe as Holy Ground and a present and future Kingdom we are building, which we will explore in Chapter Seven. Before we proceed, let us conclude our final point. We are assured that we journey out of suffering and into a life of hope by the power of prayer.

In Luke 10, Jesus sends out the expanded group of 72 disciples, granting them the power to overcome a force and adversary that seeks to diminish their current achievements and impede their future mission. He says: "I have given you authority to trample on snakes and scorpions and to overcome all the power of the enemy; nothing will harm you" (Luke 10:19, NIV). It is incredible to think that we have authority and rule from Jesus to be agents and participants in overcoming evil and providing a means for a different life for someone else! When a battle rages, when obstacles arise and when the devil seeks to throw at these precious ones what threatens to undo them, we have a role to play in meeting others' needs. We must "trample on snakes and scorpions and[...]overcome all the power of the enemy" (Luke 10:19, NIV). Snakes and scorpions are emblems of demonic power, and it is Satan's (the thief) desire to steal, kill and destroy (John 10:10). This desire also includes taking away the things that deepen your heart regarding your calling in these chapters.

I introduced this book by discussing a friend and a place using the word "hope." I did this because it is drawn from, and represents, the only source where true hope can be found. There is a well-known Old Testament verse, popular because it speaks to the craving for and seeking for what will help in our darkest moments. "For I know the plans I have for you," declares the Lord, "plans to prosper you and not to harm you, plans to give you hope and a future" (Jeremiah 29:11, NIV). I mentioned the phrase "darkest moments" because we are engaged in a battle as we walk with the poor, where we truly are overcoming the evil that challenges the idea that, for any of us who are broken, healing is a future hope. The power from God, and in the name of Jesus, is the greatest weapon against the evil that threatens to undo us or anyone we are in relationship with. It is hope grounded in prayer. Hope grounded in the power of prayer enables us to overcome all the schemes and plans of the evil one, looking toward a future that can be profoundly different for these precious ones we meet "at the table." I offer this prayer below to help ensure your ultimate heartfelt action stays steadfast:

Lord Jesus, we love you. We cherish the opportunity and ministry you provide us, along with the unique call that is ours alone. Thank you for showing what a direction toward a people in need can look like. Be with those experiencing poverty, those who call the café home, and those who are vulnerable, struggling and on the margins, wherever they may be. Keep our hearts soft now as we prepare for the upcoming call to action in the final chapter and beyond. Show us your will in guiding our hearts and in lovingly investing in the needs of those living in poverty. Most importantly, keep us surrendered to you, Lord Jesus. Free us from anything the adversary might do to dissuade us, dilute our call or prevent us from the life adventure you are inviting us into.

In your precious name we pray—Amen.

Chapter Seven

Gathered Around the Table

"The Kingdom of Heaven means the Church of Christ upon Earth, as well as the state of glory in Heaven. The one is a preparation for the other. All true Christians are heirs of God, and joint heirs with Christ, and shall inherit the glory and happiness of His Kingdom and live with Christ and be with Him forever"

—Legh Richmond, *The Annals of the Poor*[26]

The quote above refers to the Kingdom of Heaven, an intriguing and somewhat churchy phrase that embodies an idea and concept I mentioned would be part of our concluding chapter. This idea, along with some "marching orders" to come, will provide a framework for the overall final section on the call we have been exploring in serving, investing in and loving the poor.

To Walk in the Way of Holy Ground

Beloved pastor, Eugene H. Peterson (1932–2018), preached the following from one of his sermons about an idyllic place, which some considered Holy Ground:

"There was a place called Brook Farm in Massachusetts. It attracted some of ... the most famous people in New England. Among them was the ... author of the famed book-'The Scarlet Letter'- Nathaniel Hawthorne ... Hawthorne was a gloomy man ... He knew the depths of human sin and probed the dark passages of the human condition. But he must have gotten sick of it at one point and wanted out. Brook Farm promised a way out. At Brook Farm there was no sin. It was conducted on the lines of rational enlightenment (* this was an emphasis placed on reason, logic and scientific inquiry during the 17th and 18th centuries). Here people would be living at their best. At Brook Farm there was only joy and thanksgiving. (Then things fell apart—apparently not Holy Ground after all.) ... George Ripley, the guru of Brook Farm assigned Hawthorne the task of tending the manure pile. And Hawthorne didn't like it and left. He wanted Thanksgiving turkey, not chicken dung. He came to Brook Farm to live with the songs of the angels, not the refuse of the cows and the sheep."[27]

I chose the illustration of Brook Farm because it represents any "utopia" that people dream of as the perfect paradise they have been searching for, but it falls far short. This reminds me of a friend moving to Hawaii and my response about how amazing that would be. He said, "Yeah, it is beautiful and warm, but people still have to work, pay their bills, and deal with problems." So, nothing—no person, no circumstance, no place—is perfect; however, in the presence of God, we can experience Holy Ground, which means a place where God draws near, where we feel His love, and where there is a sense of otherworldliness. Amazingly, it is found as we connect with others in ways, and perhaps in places, that transcend the everyday drudgery or pain that we sometimes encounter in life.

It might be as simple as seeing something in another person that ignites a different feeling in your heart, or perhaps they have a story that resonates with yours, forging a connection. You feel compelled to learn more, to understand better, to immerse yourself in their journey and express something that could make a difference, or to share your own perspective. In those moments, whether brief or numerous, you sense that God is at work. This is the essence of Kingdom, a "thin place" where God resides. If you haven't heard this term before, a "thin place" refers to a location or experience, often described in Celtic and Christian traditions, where the veil between the spiritual and physical worlds is subtle or easily crossed, allowing a convergence of the two. The Lord's Prayer, which states "on Earth as it is in Heaven," embodies this idea. This becomes a time and space where opportunities for a deeper connection with God and the spiritual realm beyond this world are evident or possible. When I contemplate this, I envision something that moves us far beyond the ordinary—something beyond a mundane sense of church, devotion or ministry, where we become an integral part of something and where we are deeply known.

I am reminded of the words of the apostle John in his first letter where he says, "That which was from the beginning, which we have heard, which we have seen with our eyes, which we have looked at and our hands have touched—this we proclaim concerning the Word of Life" (1 John 1:1-2, NIV). The subject of these words is the experience of Jesus. This intimate depiction becomes a thin place and a space where we encounter Holy Ground when we engage with what God provides for us or invites us into. He invites us in a more personal manner that fosters a change or deepening of heart for us, and perhaps makes a difference for someone else. In this, we find the example of Jesus, who is dedicated to bringing "heaven to earth" in terms of what exists for time and eternity, which is Love. That call, which we have explored in previous chapters—the call to love, to invest, to see—is about perceiving through the eyes of Jesus.

Consider this passage:

"Jesus entered Jericho and was passing through. A man was there by the name of Zacchaeus; he was a chief tax collector and was wealthy. He wanted to see who Jesus was, but because he was short, he could not see over the crowd. So, he ran ahead and climbed a sycamore-fig tree to see him, since Jesus was coming that way. When Jesus reached the spot, he looked up and said to him, 'Zacchaeus, come down immediately. I must stay at your house today.' So, he came down at once and welcomed him gladly. All the people saw this and began to mutter, 'He has gone to be the guest of a sinner.' But Zacchaeus stood up and said to the Lord, 'Look, Lord! Here and now, I give half of my possessions to the poor, and if I have cheated anybody out of anything, I will pay back four times the amount.' Jesus said to him, 'Today salvation has come to this house, because this man, too, is a son of Abraham. For the Son of Man came to seek and to save the lost.' (Luke 19:1-10, NIV)

To see through the eyes of Jesus, we gain two insights from this story:

1. Regardless of the person, their identity, actions, or reputation, Jesus sees them with the eyes of love and value, ultimately seeing who they will become. This is the very definition of love. We see who someone is, along with all their scars, frailties and failings, and we love them anyway. We recognize their potential for growth because we also require that same reckoning and grace. I often reflect on this perspective within the context of marriage. We enter marriage not as perfect human beings but, from a Christian viewpoint, seeking holiness over happiness. This means that marriage is not a fleeting or casual undertaking; it is a commitment of sacrifice where we regard each other for who we are and where we are. Just as important (or perhaps even more so), we must see in one another and assist each other in becoming what God intended us to be. Thus, it becomes a journey for husband and wife toward greater spiritual and marital commitment, intimacy and maturity. Being transparent is a core value for me in marriage; it's not just about how my wife sees me today but also how she

perceives me as I walk this path, helping me become the man I can be in Jesus. This reflects a beautiful picture of how Jesus sees us, especially when He looks up into a tree and sees Zaccheus. To see with the eyes of Jesus, the story displays for us the reality of what being truly seen brings about in the one who experiences such love.

2. When we perceive with eyes of love and value, and envision what a person can become as they undergo this experience, there is the potential for change in how they view themselves, leading to their transformation.

Jesus looked up at him, and then, simply because he was seen, regarded and valued, Zaccheus said, "Look, Lord! Here and now, I give half of my possessions to the poor, and if I have cheated anybody out of anything, I will pay back four times the amount" (Luke 19:8, NIV). This reflects the call, power and effect of walking in the way of Holy Ground. It reflects how we see, whom we see, the love we express and the changes and responses in life that occur! To better understand the context of being engaged with God and His transformative work, we highlight how privileged we are to be part of, and witness to, God's holiness amid the brokenness we serve. Furthermore, it's essential to emphasize this truth: it's just as much for the recipient as it is for the giver. Holy Ground with Jesus involves exploring beneath the surface of what is truly happening. He presents Himself as the Living Water to everyone who seeks the truth (see John 4). By this, we mean a "seeing" where He is always aware of what is happening, ensuring that those in need receive what they require to live a different kind of life. God may have a word or message, or He may speak to you in some way about someone you know, care for or are helping. We must exercise wisdom in how this is shared, but generally, we should all remain aware as we seek investment, care, love and friendship, understanding what it means to be present in the moment while standing on Holy Ground. As we approach the end of this journey (which I hope will not be an end but a beginning), we reflect on where we have been and what will lead us to the person waiting at the table for you. Love has been our motivator, for in our calling from God, we discover who we truly are and what he asks of us.

In the café that God has clearly called us to establish, we reflect on this story from John, trusting in the imagery: in Jesus, water symbolizes spiritual refreshment and a hope for more—including eternal life. That Living Water is not just water but a source of grace that quenches the deepest spiritual thirst. And, of course, far beyond physical water, Jesus offers the only thing that will truly last! The key lesson here (we must not overlook it!) is that "at the table," people in need (which means all of us) encounter Jesus, shifting desires to the real hope that belonging can begin in community but is ultimately fulfilled in a spiritual and eternal home!

We then move from these elements of call to a clearer understanding of where, to whom, and for what purpose we are being directed. I received a message from a friend a few months ago. This friend has been a partner and a compatriot in ministry for the poor and those on the margins. He was at the church where I first tried my hand at this, and he has remained an encourager and a sounding board ever since. It's good to have someone who can help lighten the load, someone to share a laugh with. I came up with a great idea to buy a crib and fill it with baby toys, diapers and baby clothes for those in need during Christmas. I assembled the crib in our church office area (or more accurately, I tried to assemble it). My wife and anyone who knows me will tell you that "handyman" doesn't appear on my business card, so I somehow got it backward. If a child had been placed in it, that would have posed a hazard. My friend Stan pointed out the error of my ways, and we fixed it, saving a lot of embarrassment on Sunday morning. Friends... we need them.

Returning to the text, it said, "Happy New Year! It's going to be a good year! I'm focusing on more 'Bible doing.' Jesus' instructions can be found in Luke 4 and Matthew 25; thus, they are also my directives! You're my inspiration for your leadership in working with the poor and in the community." I don't quote this because the personal words make me feel good, but because they highlight how we will end this chapter. Discernment of call, motivation and direction are found in two ideas that I invite you to take with you as you leave this book: your place in God's Kingdom and the activity of building God's Kingdom; please take these as you go forward to love, invest and care. Earlier in the book, I mentioned that we would revisit the concept of Kingdom. It ties in nicely with our earlier "dream flow" of being swept into adventure and becoming part of something much larger than ourselves! As we reach our conclusion, I would like to dedicate some time to this, as I have referred to it as a thread throughout much of our discussion. What we do here helps build God's Kingdom now within our hearts and lives, and it also builds God's Heavenly Kingdom in the new Heaven and the new Earth to come.

As Jesus ministered, his teachings focused on these terms to describe God's Kingdom: Kingdom of God, Kingdom of Heaven and The Kingdom. These terms are found throughout Scripture. Jesus' teachings about what it means to build this Kingdom on Earth represent a new way of living and thinking, not a physical kingdom like a castle with walls, ramparts, a moat and a dungeon (in short, not a fairy tale). God's Kingdom is a state of reality where our hearts, lives, motivations and thus our service are centred on practicing and living out the power, truth and love of Jesus. This means that the concept of God's Kingdom is rooted in believing in a kingdom of blessing, suggesting that those who embody Kingdom principles will experience blessings in their lives. The word "blessing" can be overused. We sign emails and messages with this word; what do we mean? Blessing means being happy, content and flourishing, and this has also been a focus of this book. The degree to which we bring this level of joy and anticipation to others is the degree to which we will receive it ourselves! We derive this from a clear Biblical understanding that shows us that to be blessed is to be granted favour by God, resulting in joy, fulfillment, the living out of one's calling through spiritual gifts, and prosperity (not always necessarily financial). In the Old Testament, God's promise to Abraham serves as a foundation for blessings, which is a basis for all that is to come in the promise and Kingdom of God. As believers, we continue on this trajectory as we seek to make this world a better place by blessing the nations around us. This is where we have devised the truism, "blessed to be a blessing."

Once, when asked by the Pharisees when the Kingdom of God would come, Jesus replied, "The coming of the Kingdom of God is not something that can be observed, nor will people say, 'Here it is' or 'There it is,' because the Kingdom of God is in your midst" (Luke 17: 20-21). Thus, the message is that the Kingdom of God is not a physical entity; it represents a transformation of our hearts and minds, a way of living and believing that prepares us for eternity (see Romans 12:1-2). If you are a follower of Jesus, your citizenship is no longer 'of this world,' but your actions, behaviour, love and beliefs reflect that you are a citizen of the Heavenly Kingdom. When we say that God, his Kingdom and our allegiance to it is "not of this world," we mean that while we are present in this life, we simultaneously live in another dimension, as the aims and truths of the Kingdom do not resemble anything we find outside of God's Kingdom (see John 18:36). By aligning this with our calling to serve others and help the poor, we are building the Kingdom. The Kingdom of God signifies God's reign on Earth and in our hearts. It concerns our obedience to live the kind of life that Jesus lived and to do what He did. "Very truly I tell you, whoever believes in me will do the works I have been doing, and they will do even greater things than these" (John 14:12, NIV). Therefore, what this means as motivation to serve is that the first shall be last, the broken are blessed, we look out for our neighbour and we rejoice when the lost are found.

In summary, the Kingdom comes on Earth as it is in Heaven as each of us lives our life serving the King and serving others in the same way he did!

Marching Orders

"I am like a person going on a journey in a stagecoach, who expects its arrival every hour, and is frequently looking out the window for it[...]I am packed and sealed and ready for the post"
—John Newton (Writer of the song "Amazing Grace")[28]

When I hear a phrase, word, or message multiple times, I believe it is God speaking. The phrase I have heard is a message for you; it is your marching orders! And so now we come together and move forward, exploring once more what it means to love through our actions. My fellow travellers, you and I have walked together for some time—a rescue operation, a call, and a Kingdom. We have spent considerable time reflecting on the people God may be placing in our path, our objections about why we feel they are not meant for us, what overcoming those objections might look like (based on what God may be saying) and what passions He may be instilling in our hearts. This entire book is a story I have been unfolding, a part of my story, and He has placed it in my heart to share with you some of the most beautiful lessons, experiences and people I have ever known. I thank you for listening, and I encourage you to keep praying, thinking and reflecting on what God is saying to you, what He would like you to do about it, and what your motivation might be to come to the table!

"Jesus returned to Galilee in the power of the Spirit, and news about him spread through the whole countryside. He was teaching in their synagogues, and everyone praised him. He went to Nazareth, where he had been brought up, and on the Sabbath day, he went into the synagogue, as was his custom. He stood up to read, and the scroll of the prophet Isaiah was handed to him. Unrolling it, he found the place where it is written: 'The Spirit of the Lord is on me, because he has anointed me to proclaim good news to the poor. He has sent me to proclaim freedom for the prisoners and recovery of sight for the blind, to set the oppressed free, to proclaim the year of the Lord's favour.' Then he rolled up the scroll, gave it back to the attendant and sat down. The eyes of everyone in the synagogue were fastened on him. He began by saying to them, 'Today this Scripture is fulfilled in your hearing'" (Luke 4:14–21, NIV).

My friend said this: "Jesus' marching orders found in Luke 4 and again in Matthew 25 are my orders too!" I leave you with the marching orders from Luke 4 that Jesus quotes from the prophecy of Isaiah 61. I encourage you, no matter where you are or where you go on this walk, journey or path, or to whom God will reveal Himself to you along the way. Our great example is of course Jesus, who chose a prophetic writing to explain why He had come and selected a public and dramatic opportunity to proclaim it. As He steps into the synagogue and speaks those powerful words, He offers healing for everyone who has ever felt broken-hearted, fragmented, lost, lonely, or in distress. This is the Gospel, which means Good News, and represents everlasting healing for humanity and a doorway to heaven.

Conclusion
Tell Me a Story

As we finish this overall journey we've been on, I invite you to take a few moments for yourself to reflect on what this whole experience has been telling you about your role in all of this and where God has been speaking to your heart about your own inner love story. Find that place of love within you, consider how you are feeling, what He has been saying and what you believe and know about yourself—in truth, in identity, in value. What is your personal story of love? To what extent does the following Scripture reflect your story?

"I pray that from his glorious, unlimited resources He will empower you with inner strength through His spirit. Then Christ will make His home in your hearts as you trust in Him. Your roots will grow down into God's love and keep you strong. And may you have the power to understand, as all God's people should, how wide, how long, how high and how deep His love is. May you experience the love of Christ, though it is too great to understand fully. Then you will be made complete with all the fullness of life and power that comes from God" (Ephesians 3:16-19, NIV).

What is the role or need for love within your own story, your personal story of love, and how much do you desire for Jesus to enter all parts of this story being written? In this book, we have explored three commitments that embody the ways of love: place, community, and call. Now I conclude with the final commitment: story and storytelling.

Story and Storytelling

Stop and think for a moment: why are people drawn to stories? One reason could be that it grounds us in some way—helping us find a level of control. That is, it helps us find order in things that have happened to us, making sense of events in a random world. Stories can also let us see how others think and feel. In other words, they can allow us to empathize with the people around us. In fact, research suggests that the more compelling the story, the more empathetic people become in real life. What about yours? There are stories we tell ourselves, aren't there? Think about the inner book and chapters you've written, the "arrows" lodged in your heart, the wounds, doubts, and hurts living there. It's a self-created narrative—the person you believe you are and the things you think you'll never be able to do. You don't think about it often (or maybe you do constantly), and it's just part of you, like a second skin. You own it, live with it, and have found it a relatively tolerable way of existence, especially once you stop thinking about ever wanting to change it. Yet, it influences all you do, say and are. This may not be your story entirely, or there may be aspects of it, and it doesn't necessarily mean you've changed or healed. Still, there are truths here, which puts you in a good position to understand and minister to the people around you. As we discussed with the Book of Numbers, there's power in people's stories.

The descriptions above—the stories and narratives people have come to live with—are sometimes stories they adopt to survive. Out there, you need to understand, it's a constant effort just to survive. So, you craft a life story that helps you get by. If anyone doubts your story or questions you, you lash out because you strongly identify with it. It's your survival story! But in quieter moments, when you find some contentment in community and a sense of belonging, you reveal the true story—your genuine self. Even if it's cloaked in pain, it's still yours, and if you feel safe, you will tell it.

My late, dear friend Brad Friesen, who truly inspired me, advised me on how to walk with compassion alongside people who are living a false story—one they have chosen to survive. In response, we should do everything possible to create an environment and community where they can share their true-life narrative. Therefore, the final aspect of the way of love is to "tell me a story." The issue is that we live in a society where we can never slow down enough or care deeply enough to genuinely listen to people's stories. As Brad suggested, we build a community where people have no other agenda than to hear each other's stories. It is for this purpose, this eternal goal, that this book was written. As noted in the book's dedication, I dedicate this book to the memory of my friend. This is the story of the community we have built; I encourage you to build another—for the Glory of God and His Kingdom! Come to the table!

About the Author

Steve Griffin is the pastor of Centre for the City, at Centre Street Church in Calgary, Alberta, Canada. His vocational passion and calling is to create a place of belonging for people on the margins and for those who serve them as friends of Jesus, fostering a movement of hope. He is supported in this work by his soulmate Colette. Together, they enjoy spending time with their seven children and their families! In this work and call, they have sought to live out the redemptive promise of John 10:10: "The thief comes only to steal and kill and destroy, I have come that they might have life and have it to the full."

About PublishU

PublishU enables you to tell your story or communicate your message by writing and publishing a book worldwide.

"I never thought I would be able to write a book, let alone in 100 days... now I'm asking what else have I told myself that I can't do that I actually can?'"

PublishU Author

To find out more visit

www.PublishU.com

STEVEN P. GRIFFIN

Notes

[1] Calgary Zoo, African Savannah exhibit (2025)

[2] Service, R. W. 'The Lone Trail.', AZ Quotes, June 23, 2025, https://www.azquotes.com

/quote/898501

[3] Burnett, M. & Downey, R., directors. Son of God. 20th Century Fox, 2014.

[4] Morrell, M. & Capparell, S. Shackleton's Way: Leadership Lessons from the Great Antarctic Explorer (New York: Viking Adult, 2001).

[5] Collier, W. The Authorized Biography of Eugene H. Peterson (Colorado Springs: Waterbrook, 2021).

[6] Hickman, E. The Works of Jonathan Edwards (London: Banner of Truth Trust, 1834).

[7] Cherry-Garrard, A. The Worst Journey in the World: Antarctic 1901-1913, Vol.1 (Edinburgh: Constable, 1922).

[8] Cook, J. & Baldwin, S.C. Love, Acceptance and Forgiveness (Raleigh, N.C: Regal Books, 1982).

[9] Guidara, W. Unreasonable Hospitality (New York: Optimism Press, 2022).

[10] Desmond, M. Evicted: Poverty and Profit in the American City (Danvers: Crown, 2017).

[11] Smith, A. M. The Great Hippopotamus Hotel (New York: Penguin, 2024).

[12] Taylor, H. Mrs. Borden of Yale: The Life and Legacy of William Borden (Seattle: Aneko Press, 2024).

[13] Yankoski, M. Under the Overpass: A Journey of Faith on the Streets of America (Colorado Springs: Multnomah Books, 2005.)

[14] Morrell, M. and Capparell, S. Shackleton's Way: Leadership Lessons from the Great Antarctic Explorer (New York: Viking Adult, 2001.

[15] Hall, E.T. The Hidden Dimension (New York: Doubleday, 1966)

[16] Nouwen, H. J. M. The Only Necessary Thing: Living a Prayerful Life (New York: Crossroad Publishing, 2008).

[17] Lewis, C.S. The Collected Works of C.S. Lewis: The Pilgrim's Regress, Christian Reflections, God in the Dock (Pompano Beach: Inspirational Press, 1996.)

[18] Boas, R. A Candle in the Window. A Candle in the Window Hospitality Network, 10 June 2025, https://thewalpoleclairion.com

19 Eliot, T.S. The Waste Land: Collected Poems -1909-1962 (London: Faber and Faber, 2020).

20 Buchanan, M. God Walk: Moving at the Speed of Your Soul (Grand Rapids: Zondervan, 2020).

21 Griffin, S. P. Stuk: Helping People Find a Better End to Their Story (Seattle: Amazon, 2022).

22 Eldredge, J. & Eldredge, S. Love and War (Colorado Springs: Waterbrook Press, 2011).

23 Morrell, M & Capparell, S. Shackleton's Way: Leadership Lessons from the Great Antarctic Explorer (New York: Viking Adult, 2001).

24 Morrell, M. and Capparell, S. Shackleton's Way: Leadership Lessons from the Great Antarctic Explorer (New York: Viking Adult, 2001.

25 Zylla, P. C. The Roots of Sorrow: A Pastoral Theology of Suffering (Waco: Baylor University Press, 2012).

26 Richmond L. The Annals of the Poor (Seattle: Amazon, 2011).

27 Eugene H. Peterson, This Hallelujah Banquet, (Colorado Springs: Water BrookPress, 2021).

28 Bright, B. The Journey Home: Finishing with Joy (Nashville: Thomas Nelson, 2004.

www.ingramcontent.com/pod-product-compliance
Lightning Source LLC
La Vergne TN
LVHW052031080426
835513LV00018B/2278